ANDY WARHOL

BIG IDEAS FROM ART

Published in 2026 by The School of Life
First published in the USA in 2026
930 High Road, London, N12 9RT

Authorised representative in the EEA:
The School of Life Amsterdam, Frederiksplein 54,
1017 XN Amsterdam, Netherlands

Illustrations © Anna Doherty
Designed and typeset by Studio Katie Kerr
Printed in China by C&C Offset Printing Co., Ltd.

A proportion of this book has appeared online at www.theschooloflife.com/articles

This book is a revised and updated edition of 'What Adults Don't Know About Art'.

Every effort has been made to contact the copyright holders of the material reproduced in this book. If any have been inadvertently overlooked, the publisher will be pleased to make restitution at the earliest opportunity.

The School of Life publishes a range of books on essential topics in psychological and emotional life, including relationships, parenting, friendship, careers and fulfilment. The aim is always to help us to understand ourselves better – and thereby to grow calmer, less confused and more purposeful. Discover our full range of titles, including books for children, here: www.theschooloflife.com/books

The School of Life also offers a comprehensive therapy service, which complements, and draws upon, our published works: www.theschooloflife.com/therapy

www.theschooloflife.com

ISBN 978-1-916753-63-1

10 9 8 7 6 5 4 3 2 1

LEARNING TO APPRECIATE ART AND CREATIVITY

BIG IDEAS FROM ART

THE SCHOOL OF LIFE PRESS

THIS BOOK OF

BIG IDEAS

BELONGS TO:

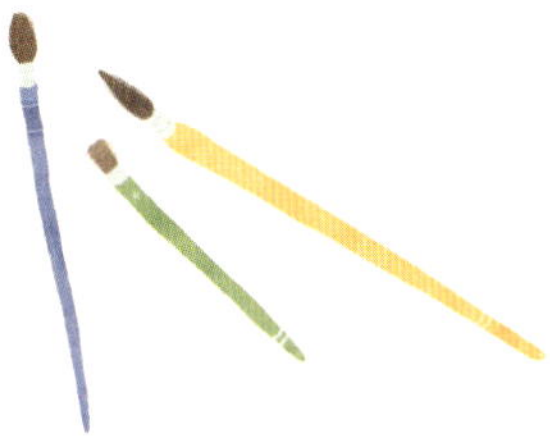

INSIDE THIS BOOK...

INTRODUCTION
WHAT IS ART? P 9

REMEMBERING P 47

SADNESS P 111

APPRECIATION P 67

BALANCE P 127

HOPE P 93

MAKING SENSE OF MONEY P 145

CONCLUSION
ART IN YOUR LIFE P 163

WHAT IS ART?

You and Art

You have probably been interested in art for a long time. Perhaps it began even earlier than you remember, with the first scribbles you made one afternoon when you were in the kitchen and someone handed you coloured pens and a big sheet of paper. You weren't trying to draw anything in particular – you were just seeing what happened when colour met paper.

Can you picture the first piece of art you were really proud of? What did it show? Your parents probably stuck it on the fridge or even framed it. It might have looked something like this – bright, colourful and full of joy.

Do you remember how it felt when you were creating it? How hard you tried to pick just the right colours to recreate what was in your imagination. You really enjoyed colouring the clouds blue and you were pleased with the yellow house. Dad said he liked the kite in the picture.

And of course, you didn't only make art; you also started to see it. Maybe the first art you really liked was a picture in a book. It showed you exactly what the story was telling you, so you could imagine it so clearly. Maybe you thought it would be fun to be there with a big friendly tiger drinking from a teapot, a mischievous rabbit sneaking into a neighbour's garden, or a very hungry caterpillar searching for something to eat.

Probably no one told you these pictures were art. But they were made by artists – people using colours and shapes to tell stories, just like you once did with your first drawings. They are art – and they are fun, interesting and important to you.

Then, as you got older, you might have come across art in a very different kind of place. Maybe you even went on a trip to a museum or gallery when you were on holiday or on a school trip. The museum was huge, with lots of people – maybe you kept worrying someone was going to bump into you. It was exciting, but also a bit overwhelming – there was so much to look at, and every picture raised another question. Nobody said very much and when they talked, they spoke quietly. It felt like a very grown-up place where you had to be on your best behaviour.

You weren't allowed to run about and definitely couldn't touch anything. There might have been lots of different pictures on the walls that you couldn't make much sense of.

Maybe you saw a painting like the one on the next page. Looking at this picture, you might wonder why that little boy's mum is standing on a carved stone, or why the children with wings are holding her legs. Is she going to fall off? The wings – and the fact they aren't wearing any clothes – look a bit strange too. They're meant to show that these are angels, not ordinary children.

Andrea del Sarto, *Madonna of the Harpies*, 1517

And not every artwork even looked like a picture at all. Perhaps you saw something a bit like this. It sort of looks like a table ... but don't try putting a glass of orange juice on it or else an alarm will ring, and the guards will be very angry! Though it looks like furniture, this is art, too. Brancusi called it *Fish* because he was trying to capture in the shapes of the sculpture the feeling of how a fish moves – smooth and quick, its shiny body flashing through the water.

A lot of art is pictures and paintings, but there are plenty of other kinds of art too, like sculpture, textiles and installation.

Constantin Brancusi, *Fish*, 1926

Most of the time, though, when you were in the museum, you might have just seen the backs of people who were standing in the way. And when you overheard grown-ups talking about these pieces of art, it might have sounded complicated and not really connected to you.

Grown-ups want you to go to art galleries and museums, even if they don't go to them very often themselves. But many of them have forgotten that art isn't only found in special buildings – it's all around us in ordinary places, too.

The Big Question No One Answers (Until Now)

If you ask someone, 'Is art important?', they will probably say, 'Yes, it's very important.' But suppose you ask a bigger question. Suppose you ask, '*Why* is it important?' What might people say if you ask this? They might not find it easy to answer. Some might say, 'Because it's very old.'

But this isn't a very good answer, because a stone is very old too – actually much, much older than any work of art – and no one asks you to go and admire a pebble. And your grandad is probably quite old, but no one wants to put him in an art gallery! There must be more to it than that.

Old artworks can give us a glimpse into how people lived in the past. They can show us what people wore, what they cared about and even what they feared. They help us understand history and the people who came before us.

So, art could be important because it's old. But some art isn't old at all, some is younger than you are. What else makes art important?

Others might say, 'Because it looks so real.'

But that isn't a great answer either. All the photos on a phone look real too, and adults are always telling kids to get off their phones. And anyway, lots of art doesn't look very real at all.

Or someone might say, 'Because it costs a lot.'

It's true that some famous artworks cost millions. But that's not the most convincing reason for why art matters. There are plenty of things in the world that are very expensive, like oil tankers. But grown-ups don't go around saying how wonderful oil tankers are or put them in special buildings in the middle of big cities where you can go and look at them. And no one worries that your school doesn't spend enough time teaching you about container vessels.

Most art in the world costs much less than that – and some of it, like your own drawings, costs nothing at all. The price of something doesn't make it art. What makes it art is the person who created it and what they were trying to express.

In short, even though lots of people say that art is important, they often find it hard to explain why. But maybe it's not very fair to expect all grown-ups to know why art is important. There are lots of things the grown-ups you know don't understand, but that doesn't mean there is not a good answer. They don't know (really) how their phone works, but someone, somewhere, knows perfectly well.

So perhaps the answer could be in a book about art. There are lots of books about art, so surely one of them must cover it. But actually, most art books do not tell you why art matters. They tell you what the famous pictures are.

But fame isn't a very helpful reason for why something should matter to you. Just because something is famous doesn't mean you should be interested in it.

It would be a bit surprising if the grown-ups said: 'We have to take some trips to visit famous airports! We'll start with Heathrow and then maybe go and see Schiphol – it's one of the most famous airports in Europe.' Or imagine if your mum said: 'I want to go to Chile so I can see the Escondida copper mine. It's the most famous copper mine in the world!'

If they're not talking about which pictures are famous, books about art usually tell you who the great artists are. They will probably mention some of these people:

PABLO PICASSO

FRIDA KAHLO

ANDY WARHOL

CLAUDE MONET

GEORGIA O'KEEFFE

YAYOI KUSAMA

But going through names is not actually a very convincing answer to the question of why we should care about art. And most art books focus on only one kind of art, usually painting, even though art includes many other techniques as well.

You could find a book to tell you who the great dentists or great dog trainers in the world are. Or you could make a list of the people who have had the greatest influence in the development of fridges and freezers:

WILLIAM CULLEN

CARL VON LINDE

BEULAH LOUISE HENRY

Usually, your school and family are not trying to get you interested in fridge and freezer people. Of course, it's really great that these people helped us keep our vegetables fresh, but we don't need to spend a lot of time finding out about them. You could be completely fine if you never heard another word about them in your life.

So, even though we have asked adults and looked in books about art, we still haven't got an answer to the big question: *Why is art important?*

Books and people say art is important, but they don't say *why*. This can feel a bit strange. You're used to adults having answers for lots of things – even if they don't always explain those answers to you. But sometimes, if you really push for an answer, you realise that no one has a simple one to give.

But maybe this isn't so unusual. There are plenty of important questions adults haven't solved. For instance: *How can you make a big city beautiful?*

No one really knows the answer to this – which is why most large cities have some lovely parts and some not so nice parts. Or: *What's the best way to organise a school?* Perhaps hardly anyone seems sure because there are only a few truly brilliant schools.

It's not that there can't be good answers to these questions. It's just that people have not worked them out yet. So maybe it's the same with art. It's not that there isn't a good answer to the big question; it's just that we haven't found it yet.

In this book, we are going to be doing something new and unusual. We're going to look for an answer to a big question: why might some works of art be important to *you*?

It's a bit like being an explorer. There were the first people to go to the North Pole, then the first people to climb to the top of Mount Everest, and then the first people to walk on the moon.

The same sort of thing can happen with questions and ideas. We're going to explore this big question for the first time, together, in this book. We are adventurers in big ideas.

Why your Bedroom Is An Art Gallery

We have talked about big art galleries with lots of people and lots of paintings hung on the walls in ornate frames. But to understand why art is important to you, we need to think about a place that feels like the complete opposite of an art gallery. Think about your ideal bedroom. Imagine you've got a new bedroom, and you can put anything on the walls. It's just for you – no one is going to complain or say you can't do something or that anything is silly. It's your space. It's totally up to you. What would you put up? Maybe some things like these:

You put up posters because you like looking at them and because they show things that mean a lot to you. Your room is an exciting and important place: it reflects your life and your personality. All around you are reminders of the people you love, the things you enjoy, and the experiences you've had. It might be, for you, the nicest room in the world.

The Tribuna of the Uffizi gallery, Florence, Italy

Compare this art gallery to your room. You have just got some posters stuck up with pins or sticky tape, and the gallery has paintings that are hundreds of years old in golden frames. Your room has a bed in it, but this place has marble statues instead – and there's definitely nowhere to hang your clothes.

The Tribuna of the Uffizi gallery in Florence, Italy, is one of the oldest and most famous rooms for art in the world. 'Uffizi' means 'the offices' because a long time ago it was built above the offices of a bank. You have to queue for hours just to get in. People travel from all over the world to visit.

If you look closely at the picture, you can see statues of ancient Roman heroes and paintings of scenes from myths and history. They're arranged in a grand circle, almost like treasures displayed in someone's very fancy sitting room.

But in an important way, your ideal room and this gallery are the same. Works of art are really just special pictures that other people have wanted to put in *their* rooms. And your room is really a private version of a gallery – a place filled with posters and objects that matter to you.

This isn't so strange. A lot of famous galleries actually started out as private rooms that belonged to wealthy families, kings, or queens.

In 1813, an architect called John Soane reorganised this room in his home in London. It was his favourite room in the house. He hung all his favourite paintings and drawings on the walls and he put his favourite books in the bookcases. There are interesting shells he collected in the room, too, because he liked their shapes and colours, and there are models of buildings he liked. For him, everything in the room had a very personal meaning: a little drawing of a place he liked to go on holiday, or of somewhere he wanted to go but never got the chance to visit (Soane dreamt of going to Egypt, but it was extremely difficult to travel there in the 19th century); some books with illustrations he loved looking at; a special fossil he picked up while out for a walk.

Sir John Soane's Museum, Lincoln's Inn Fields, London

John liked having his breakfast in this room. But you can't eat a slice of toast in it these days because it's been turned into an art gallery. He died in 1837, but we hope that he'd be happy that other people are still appreciating his special room and quietly admiring the works of art that were so important to him.

Even if an art gallery didn't actually begin as someone's house, a lot of the art on the walls really did start out as things people had in their own rooms. When people wanted to share these special works with more than just the visitors to their homes, they sometimes sold them or donated them to galleries so that everyone could enjoy them. That is how many famous artworks ended up in museums.

This picture was a special artwork for the King's bedroom:

Anthony Van Dyck, *Charles I (1600–1649) with M. de St Antoine*, 1633

The man on the horse is King Charles I of England. The picture was painted by his friend Anthony van Dyck in 1633. Sometimes the King rode his horse right into his palace. He was the King, so no one could say, 'Charles, I've told you before, don't ride your horse in the house, you'll get mud all over the carpet!'

Because he was a king, he didn't buy this artwork in a shop; he asked a famous artist to make one especially for him. And he needed a huge room too, because the picture is about 3.5 metres high.

In the same way as King Charles had an enormous and very expensive portrait of himself in his room, other people might have had special pictures of their relatives hung in theirs – just like your grandparents might have a photo of you when you were little. But before cameras were invented, people used paintings and drawings to remind them of the people they loved.

Titian, *Clarissa Strozzi (1540-1581)*, 1542

This little girl was called Clarissa. Her parents had to move far away, so they had this picture painted so that Clarissa's aunts and uncles could see what she looked like. It was painted nearly five hundred years ago by the most famous artist in the world at that time, a man called Titian.

Or maybe, instead of admiring musicians or sports stars and having posters of them on their walls, someone might have wanted something to remind them of their favourite stories. Ancient Greek and Roman myths were especially popular for centuries, so people sometimes asked artists to paint them a picture of the most exciting moment in the story.

In the past, some of the most loved stories in the world were about a man called Ulysses. This painting shows the moment when Ulysses and his friends land on an island.

J.M.W. Turner, *Ulysses deriding Polyphemus*, 1829

This island seems great – but it's actually inhabited by one-eyed giants. One of the giants captures them and keeps them in his cave. They think they've had it, but Ulysses comes up with a clever plan.

The giant owns sheep that sleep in the cave. When he lets them out in the morning, Ulysses and his friends hide amongst the flock and escape back to their ship. The giant realises they've escaped. He throws enormous rocks at them (you can just about see the giant's head and shoulders emerging behind the hill), but they miss the boat.

Then the giant shouts out to Ulysses, 'What's your name?' And Ulysses, thinking fast, shouts in reply, 'I'm nobody.'

The giant, not being very clever, calls out to the other giants, 'Help! Nobody is escaping!' And of course, the other giants don't come to help – since nobody is escaping. Ulysses and his friends are safe, and they head off to their next exciting adventure.

People made their own posters, too. This one is by Vincent van Gogh, a famous painter who lived in the 19th century. It's a picture of his friend Eugène Boch.

Vincent van Gogh, *Portrait of Eugène Boch*, 1888

Eugène's family owned a factory, and they were very wealthy, but Eugène himself was an artist – a painter who belonged to a group of artists in Belgium. His sister, Anna, was a painter too, and the two of them got on well. Eugène spent a lot of time with other artists, and he often helped them if they were short of money (which they often were). He and van Gogh became good friends, and van Gogh painted this picture of him.

This was van Gogh's bedroom when he was living in Arles, in the south of France. He liked it so much he painted several paintings of it. This is the first one he did in 1888.

Vincent van Gogh, *The Bedroom*, 1888

After Vincent van Gogh finished the portrait of Eugène Boch, he hung it in his bedroom. And then he painted this picture – of his bedroom with this painting in it!

You can just about see the picture of his friend Eugène, in his yellow jacket, hanging above the bed.

It would be amazing if Vincent had hung this picture of his bedroom in his bedroom – and then made another picture of that, and hung that one up, and then made a picture of the next one, and hung that up ... But we'll make our heads hurt if we think about this too much.

In around 1660, the English artist Mary Beale wanted a picture of her son Bartholomew, so she made one herself. Bartholomew was about five when his mother painted him. They were living in London at the time, but later Mary earned money from selling her paintings and the family moved to a nice house in the countryside. When he grew up, Bartholomew became a doctor.

Mary Beale, *Sketch of the Artist's Son, Bartholomew Beale, Facing Left*, c. 1660

She made the picture because she knew that one day her son would grow up and change. He'd still be nice, but he would be different, and she wanted to remember what he looked like when he was little. It would be nice for him, too. In those days, unless someone painted a picture of you when you were small (which was very rare), you would never know what you had looked like.

Today, all these special artworks are in galleries or museums where many people can see them. But they didn't start out that way. They began as things that someone once chose to have in their own room – just as you choose what to put on the walls of yours. When you think about it, by being interested in decorating your bedroom, you're doing something similar to what people have always done with art in the past: surrounding yourself with images and objects that feel meaningful to you.

So, there are some very important questions you can ask about any work of art when you go to a gallery:

Why did the artist choose this subject?

Who was this artwork made for – themselves,
a friend, a family member, or someone important?
What might they have liked about it, and why?

What might it be like to have this artwork in your room?
Would you enjoy looking at it every day? Why or why not?

Now we're ready to answer the big question. Remember, the question isn't 'What are the most famous works of art?' or 'Who are the greatest artists?' It is a much more important question than that – it's a question about you. The big question is:

Why is art important to you?

One answer is this: a work of art is important to you if it means something – if it reminds you of something you care about, makes you feel something or if it's something you'd like to have in your ideal room.

An art gallery can be important to you because understanding the art you choose for your own space helps you make sense of the art you find there. It might also contain suggestions about what you might like to have in your room.

All the people who have made and collected art are speaking to you. They're saying: *Here are the things that meant something to us. We liked displaying these things in our rooms. Maybe there's something here that might excite you as well.*

Most of the art in the world won't excite you, and that's completely fine. You don't have to like everything, and you do not need to have a huge number of things in your room. You just need to find the few things that feel meaningful to you.

Finding these things is a project that you are starting right now, and that can go on for the whole of your life.

Why Art Galleries Are Boring

We've been saying that art has a lot to do with your ideal room – a place where you can keep the things you like that hold meaning to you. But sometimes real art galleries can feel quite different. You might enjoy thinking about what you'd put on your own walls, but standing in a gallery can feel quite dull, confusing, or even a bit overwhelming.

One reason is that galleries can sometimes seem very serious. If you're in a gallery you can usually see little notes next to the works of art. Often these are helpful – they might tell you the artist's name, the title of the picture and when it was made. You might notice adults looking at them very carefully, with serious expressions on their faces, as if they are studying for an exam.

Let's take the picture on the next page, for instance. Even without knowing anything about it, you might enjoy the soft trees, the glowing sky or the different shades of green. Claude Lorrain was famous for painting hills and valleys, but he wasn't very good at painting people. The heads looked too small, and the limbs weren't quite right.

Claude Lorrain, *Landscape with David at the Cave of Adullam*, 1658

Here's the label that might go beside it:

Claude Lorrain (1600–1682)
Landscape with David at the Cave of Adullam, 1658,
Oil on canvas

Painted in 1658 for Prince Agostino Chigi (1634–1705), this work depicts King David with his followers outside the Cave of Adullam. David longed for water from the well of Bethlehem. Three mighty men broke through the army of the Philistines to fetch the water for him. When they returned, David realised he had unnecessarily risked their lives and instead poured the water out for the Lord (2 Samuel 23: 13–17). A number of preparatory drawings by Claude are known.

Reading this label can make you feel as if you're supposed to know lots of facts before you're allowed to enjoy the picture – almost as if you're preparing for an exam. And if you are going to pass, you'll need to answer these questions. Are you ready? You're not allowed to look at the label again – no cheating!

QUESTION:
Who painted this picture?
ANSWER:
Someone called Claude Lorrain.

Well done, that was on the label. Good memory!

QUESTION:
Who was Agostino Chigi?
ANSWER:
A prince.

That's right – the label says he was a prince. But do you know anything else about him? If you asked a million adults, it would be amazing if even one of them had heard of him.

QUESTION:
When was it painted?
ANSWER:
1658.

But that doesn't help much unless you already know about other things that happened then.

QUESTION:
Why is it important that 'a number of preparatory drawings by Claude are known'?
ANSWER:
Because it proves that this picture really was painted by Claude Lorrain, not by someone else.

Were you thinking: 'Oh I really, really hope this is by someone called Claude and not by someone else I've never heard of?' Be honest ...

QUESTION:
What is (2 Samuel 23: 13–17)?
ANSWER:
It refers to a story in the Bible.

The label expects you to know this. But very few people know this story.

Maybe it's not surprising that a lot of people are very quiet in art galleries: they're worried someone is going to ask them some very hard questions they don't know the answers to. It can feel a bit daunting and off-putting. All this seriousness and all these facts can make you feel that you don't know anything at all – as if not knowing all the names and dates means you've no business looking at pictures.

But there's good news. None of this really matters very much. Remember, you're trying to find something for your ideal room – something you love and want to have around you for a long time. The exam-style questions don't help you love the picture.

Loving a work of art is a bit like making a new friend. You become friends with someone because you like doing things with them. You like playing football with them or joking with them or going to the park together.

It'd be astonishing if people said you couldn't be friends with someone unless you took an exam about them first, showing you know what year their mum was born or what their dad's middle name is. You might find out these things later, but they are nothing at all to do with *why* you like your friend.

It's the same with art. You don't like a picture because you know every fact about it. You like it because there is something in it that feels friendly to you – something that makes you smile, or think, or wonder. Just like how there might be one thing you really love about your friend, maybe there is just one part of the picture that especially interests you.

Lorrain loved clambering up the steep sides of hills, holding on to the branches of trees. In this picture, it's great how you can see through the arch in the cliff to see the light on the rock behind. You can imagine climbing up there. Be careful you don't fall! Maybe there's a cave where you could have a picnic? Art isn't really boring. But it can be made boring if it becomes an exam.

Detail from: Claude Lorrain, *Landscape with David at the Cave of Adullam*, 1658

Why a Work of Art is Like a Tool

So far, we've talked about how choosing posters to decorate your ideal room is a very helpful way to understand art and why it's important. But there's another big idea that can help too, and it might be unexpected: a work of art is a kind of tool.

Jean-François Millet, *The Wood Sawyers*, 1850–1852

That might sound a bit strange at first, because normally we think of tools as things that help our bodies do jobs. Our hands are really bad at carrying water, so someone invented a tool – a bucket – to help us with the job. It is impossible to cut wood with your fingers (please don't try!), so people invented saws, which are much better at the task.

But there are other tools that help our minds instead of our bodies. For example, imagine your dad is going to the shops. He might forget what to buy because brains aren't very good at remembering long lists. He needs a special kind of brain tool: a shopping list. That way he'll be sure to get the frozen peas and the milk. (He doesn't really need to add chocolate biscuits to the list because he never forgets those ...)

There are actually quite a lot of different brain tools:

CALCULATORS

Because even though we can work out what 113×92 is on paper, it takes time – and a calculator does it instantly. (It's 10,396, in case you were wondering.)

CLOCKS

Because our brains aren't always very good at guessing the exact time.

MAPS

Because we aren't good at working out directions on our own. A map helps us see where things are and how they connect.

While these are all important, some of the most interesting and useful brain tools are actually works of art.

Art can be a tool for many things:

Remembering
Appreciation
Hope
Sadness
Balance
Making sense of money

Maybe it doesn't feel obvious just yet how art can be a tool for these things, or why you need these tools, or even what 'appreciation' and 'balance' mean and have to do with you. In the next chapters we'll explain them. Let's get started!

CHAPTER ONE

REMEMBERING

Remembering

We can't remember everything. That's normal – nobody can. It's not that you forget your name or address or what 8+7 is ... hopefully! But there are other memories that quite easily slip away without you noticing.

You might remember some things about your sixth birthday, but lots of details get lost. Maybe at one point during that day, your dad smiled at you in a really special way – he was thinking of the day you were born, exactly six years earlier. He hardly ever smiles in exactly that way. It would be a lovely thing to remember, but it has probably disappeared.

Or perhaps there was a moment when you were opening an exciting present, and your little sister was excited because *you* were excited. It would be good to remember that moment, because sometimes sisters can be quite annoying and that moment would remind you how much your happiness means to her. But that memory has gone, too.

Your mind is a bit like a big messy cupboard. There are loads of interesting things inside it, but some things get pushed to the back, where you can't easily find them. It's the same with memories. There are lots of memories in your 'mind-cupboard', but a lot of them get hidden away in the corners, so you hardly even realise they are there. But if you could access those lost memories, they could be wonderful and really useful. That's where art can help.

Art is a tool for remembering. A picture can help you to keep a memory near the front of your mind so you can get to it quickly – whether it's a memory the artist wanted to save or a memory you have when you look at the picture.

John Singer Sargent, *The Birthday Party*, 1887

Here's a story about how art began. Art has been around for a very, very long time and nobody really knows how it started. One idea is that people began making art because they wanted to remember things.

Long ago, in ancient Greece, there was a boy who was a shepherd. He was good friends with a girl who lived in the same village. During the winter and spring, they could see each other practically every day, go for walks and have long chats together.

But then the summer came round. That was a big problem. In those days, in summer, shepherds would have to take their sheep far away, up to the mountains to feed on the new grass. This meant that the shepherd boy and his friend wouldn't see each other for months.

On the last day before the boy had to leave, he was sitting together with the girl feeling sad, and she noticed his shadow on the wall. She picked up a soft bit of stone and started tracing the outline of his shadow. She made a picture of him so she wouldn't forget him while he was away.

This moment was so powerful that, thousands of years later, another artist painted *this* picture to help us remember it. And it tells us something important: a picture doesn't only help one person remember – it can help lots of people remember a moment, an idea or a story from long ago.

Jean-Baptiste Regnault, *The Origin of Painting: Dibutades Tracing the Portrait of a Shepherd*, 1785

It is why your granny likes to have photos of you. There are lots of things that you might try to remember. Some artists are interested in making memory-pictures of special moments in their children's lives. And like the ancient story we've just seen, these pictures don't only help the artist remember – they can help us remember moments, feelings or ideas that might otherwise slip away.

Thomas Gainsborough, *The Painter's Daughters Chasing a Butterfly*, c. 1756

One evening, a very long time ago back in 1756, Thomas Gainsborough's two young daughters were in the garden. It was getting late, and they'd been told they had to go back indoors. Then the little one saw a white butterfly beside them.

She was filled with wonder at this beautiful, strange creature fluttering right past her and she wanted to hold it, but her big sister said they had to go in (even though she was quite interested in the butterfly as well). It was a lovely moment.

Gainsborough was one of the most successful portrait painters in 18th century England. He specialised in painting pictures of very wealthy people looking elegant and serious (which they weren't always in real life). Sometimes for himself, he also painted pictures of his family, like this one of his daughters. Gainsborough decided to paint a picture so that he'd always remember that moment. When you're six or seven you think you'll stay like that forever, but Gainsborough knew his daughters would grow up, and they might not remember this special moment. Just like a butterfly, the memory is there for a moment, then you never see it again.

Imagine what it would have been like for the little girls, when they were older, to look back at this picture. In those days, photographs hadn't been invented yet, and hardly anyone ever got to see a picture of themselves when they were young. But even today, when we can take photos all the time, art can help us remember things in a different way – not just what something looked like, but what it *felt* like. If you could ask an artist to help you remember some special moments in your life, what might they be? Don't worry if you can't think of any straight away – maybe you'll think of your answer tomorrow, or next week or even next year.

It isn't just nice moments with people that you might want to remember, though. You might want to remember a place, somewhere interesting you went on holiday or even a really amazing view.

Imagine that you went on a holiday to Japan (a lot of thinking involves imagining things!). You might go on a super-fast train and see Mount Fuji. That would be great. But for you, that might not be the most important thing that happens. Instead, it might be that one day there was a lot of mist, and it looked really beautiful.

More than four hundred years ago, there lived a Japanese artist called Hasegawa Tōhaku. He loved misty days too. He liked how you could look into the forest and just see a few of the trees through the thick white air – if you took two steps back some of the trees would completely disappear, and if you took two steps forward you would see some more start to emerge. He wanted to remember the strange, magical feeling of those misty moments, so Tōhaku made a picture to help him remember what it was like (because usually it wasn't misty).

Hasegawa Tōhaku, *Pine Trees / left hand screen*, 16th century

You might imagine art as things in frames that you hang on a wall. But in Japan, a lot of art was painted on tall folding screens as high as a person. Each of the vertical lines in the picture is actually a joint. The screens could be folded so that they could stand up on their own and moved around a room.

One painter in history really liked muddy fields, especially in the evening. On one particular day it had been raining nonstop, and then the sun came out. There was a beautiful sunset. He went out for a walk, and while he was out, he saw a muddy field. Looking at the field, he felt small and the world seemed very big, but in a lovely way. He didn't want to forget that place or that feeling, so he painted the picture on the next page.

Caspar David Friedrich, *The Grosse Gehege near Dresden*, c. 1832

Caspar David Friedrich lived in Germany in the 19th century. He loved taking long walks alone in the countryside. His favourite times of day were dawn and dusk. Friedrich felt that nature was speaking to him about his life.

The mist or a puddle might not be exactly what you want to remember. But hopefully they give you some suggestions about things that could be important to you. What's your version of a muddy puddle or seeing a tree through the mist? What do you like to look at, and remember?

Sometimes the memory that you want to hold on to is not a person or a place – it's the way you feel. Some feelings are so special, or so unusual, that you want to remember what they were like. That's what this next picture is doing: it's capturing a mood or a feeling so it doesn't disappear.

The picture was painted by Hilaire-Germain-Edgar Degas. Degas was born in France in 1834. His family was quite rich, and his father wanted him to be a lawyer or a banker, but he chose to be an artist instead. He lived in America, then he moved to Paris. He often went on holiday to the seaside.

Hilaire-Germain-Edgar Degas, *Beach Scene*, c. 1869–1870

In the picture, the other children have gone swimming, but the girl under the umbrella is feeling quieter and more dreamy. Her swimming costume is drying beside her (that brown suit laid out on the right – that's what swimsuits looked like in those days). Maybe she feels a bit tired from being in the water, or just wants to lie on the sand, look up at the sky and wonder about things. You can imagine that she was having interesting thoughts:

I'm still tired from swimming ...
I like watching the waves from here ...
Maybe I don't quite know what I want to do ...

How do people find out what to do?
What might my life be like when I am grown-up?
How will I change in the future?

Perhaps you sometimes feel like this too. It's an important mood: your mind is starting to explore some big, difficult, fascinating questions.

As well as making pictures of people, places or things that capture a certain mood, there's another way artists can help you remember a feeling: they can make an 'abstract' picture. It's called 'abstract' because it doesn't look like anything you normally see. It's a picture of what a feeling *feels* like.

There are times when you're feeling bouncy and happy, like maybe you want to jump around a bit. That might be how the artist was feeling when they painted this picture. They put vivid colours together to make a bright, abstract painting.

But even though you do feel ecstatic sometimes, feelings change, and you won't always be in such a jolly mood. When you look at a picture like this it reminds you of the happy feeling you had, and maybe helps it come back.

Cy Twombly, who painted this picture, was born in Virginia in the US in 1928. His father was a famous baseball player. He knew he wanted to be an artist from the age of twelve. Though people said his style was new and shocking, he often got his ideas by studying very old things, like ancient Greek myths.

Cy Twombly, *Untitled*, 2001

Art can also be used to remember an idea. One day, a very long time ago in the 14th century, the ruler of Japan knocked over a bowl. It fell on the floor and broke into pieces. It was a simple bowl, but he liked it very much: he used to drink his favourite tea from it every day. He was very upset. Instead of just throwing the broken pieces away and getting a new bowl, one of his assistants came up with a clever idea. They would mend the bowl in a very special way, by using gold to join the pieces back together. It was very tricky to do, but in the end they managed it. The bowl looked even more beautiful than before: it had become a work of art.

The ruler was so pleased that they made up a special name for this way of mending things. They called it *kintsugi*. *Kin* means 'golden' in Japanese and *tsugi* means 'joinery' or putting things together. So kintsugi means 'mending with gold'.

Kintsugi represents an important idea: that broken things can be repaired – and sometimes, after they've been mended, they can be even more special than they were before. You can still see where it was broken, but now you don't mind – the golden lines make the cracks part of the story.

And this isn't just a lesson about bowls. It's also a lesson about art – and life. In art, things don't have to be perfect to be beautiful: a smudge, a slip or a mistake can turn into something interesting. Sometimes the thing that went 'wrong' becomes the best part.

It is not just bowls that can get broken. A friendship might get damaged – someone might say something not very nice and you feel let down or upset. Maybe you feel like throwing the broken friendship away. Or maybe sometimes *you* feel a bit broken yourself. Everything seems to be going wrong and you just want to give up.

But kintsugi teaches us that as well as bowls, friendships and people can be mended and become stronger than before. Saying sorry or forgiving someone strengthens a friendship. It does not pretend that nothing happened; it adds something precious on top of the cracks. And if you let someone help you when you're struggling, you can become stronger too.

Kintsugi is a tricky idea, and easy to forget. It gets hidden away at the back of your mind-cupboard. But if you look at the bowl mended with gold, it will help you remember the idea: mistakes, breakages and difficult moments can be part of what makes something – or someone – truly special.

Another idea we often forget about is luck. There are all sorts of things we can't control, and they make a big difference to how our lives turn out. You might be quite good at maths or running fast – but you didn't make your body or your brain yourself. Other people might struggle with those things, but it's not their fault.

Remembering about luck helps us to be kinder and more understanding. When we forget about it, we can start to feel proud or think we're better than others or take things for granted. When we remember it, we're kinder to others and grateful for our own good fortune.

The picture on the next page helps keep the idea of luck at the front of our minds. It is a page from an illustrated medieval book. There was no printing back then, so every book had to be copied out and illustrated by hand, which took ages. Hardly anyone had books at home – not even one. This book was written in the 1300s; it tells the life stories of famous people.

The big wheel lifts people up and then, as it turns, it brings them down again. The people on it haven't necessarily done anything very special or very bad – the wheel just turns. Their lives go well for a while, then go badly, and then maybe go well again.

It is helpful to remember that things in life can change: sometimes we're lucky, and sometimes we're not, and we can't control everything. Art like this can help us keep that thought in our mind when we are going about our daily lives.

OPPOSITE:
French School (15th century), *Dame Fortune and Victims Falling from her Wheel*, from Boccaccio's *The Fall of Princes*, 1467

Selon raison et bonnes
meurs lomme soy con
versant en aucune sci
ence speculatiue ou
aultre puet honneste
ment muer son con
seil ou propos de bien
en mieulx attendue la mutacion des cho
ses et des temps et des lieux Et aussy
puet ung potier casser et rompre aucu
sien vaissel combien quil soit bien fait
pour lui donner aultre forme qui lui
semble meilleur Et ceste licence de
muer la chose en mieulx nest pas
donnee a lomme pour seulement ame
der ou corrigier sa propre oeuvre ains
mesmement leist a chun de ce faire
en la besongne dautrui puisque on la
face par bonte de couraige et par mou
uement de vraie charite qui en soy ne
contient envie ne arrogance Com
me doncques ja pieca je laurens de pre
mier fait a lenhortement et requeste
daucuns eusse translate de latin en
francois le moins mal que jay peu
ung tresnotable et exquis livre de
Jehan Boccace des cas des nobles ho
mes et femes En la translacion du

The idea that this painting below is helping us to remember is really important (and really easy to forget). The painter, Berthe Morisot, hasn't put in all the details – you can't really see people's faces, for instance. She wasn't being lazy. She wanted us to feel how nice it is in the countryside without being distracted by thinking about who these people are. This type of painting is called Impressionism.

The painting shows a lovely moment: everyone was happy, but nothing much was going on. They were just sitting in a field near some trees. They weren't buying nice things or going to a party. We often forget that usually it is very simple and ordinary things like this that actually make us happy.

Berthe Morisot, *In a Park*, c. 1874

Good ideas can help us to be kinder and wiser, but we're not very good at keeping the important ideas at the front of our mind-cupboards. That's why we need the right works of art around us (in our rooms) to remind us. Your room – your gallery – is a kind of remembering machine, just for you. When you are deciding what you want to have in your room, one of the questions you are asking yourself is: *What do I want to remember?*

And if you are visiting a gallery, or if you are looking at a book of pictures, you are asking yourself: *Are there any clues here about what it would be good for me to remember? And what should I keep right at the front of my mind-cupboard?*

Try this: Pick one moment, place, feeling or idea from your own life that you'd like to remember. How could you draw or paint it so that your future self would recognise the feeling inside it?

CHAPTER TWO

APPRECIATION

Appreciation

Appreciation is quite a serious, grown-up word: it might not be one you use much (or at all). But it's a helpful word because when you appreciate something, it's the opposite of finding it boring. Art can help you to appreciate people and things – especially the small things that are easy to overlook.

Let's start with a problem: feeling bored. Maybe you get bored quite a lot – practically everyone does. You look around your life and it all seems so familiar, just the same old stuff. Why doesn't anything exciting happen?

You probably have all sorts of ideas about what would be exciting. Imagine if a dinosaur walked past the window ... Or if you could blast off into space in a rocket? It would be great if you had a pet penguin. Or a cute koala. But obviously nothing like this is really going to happen. Life can feel so dull!

Remember we've been saying that works of art are brain tools? Well, one of the things they can do is help your brain notice how interesting ordinary things really are. Sometimes the small things turn out to be the most joyful ones – if you look at them the right way.

Let's look at how that can happen. We can start with something that might sound very boring indeed: grass. There's lots of grass around. It's green. You might think grass could be just about the least interesting thing in the whole world.

Let's look at an artist who looked at grass very carefully. In Albrecht Dürer's picture of grass on the next page, each blade is different. You could imagine being a tiny insect wandering around looking for lunch; it would be like being in a huge jungle. You could make a little house and become friends with a ladybird. You might get chased by a worm (luckily worms are slow).

Dürer started learning to be an artist when he was a child and became famous when he was in his twenties. He was the first person in all of Europe to draw a rhinoceros – but it wasn't very accurate because he'd never actually seen one!

What Dürer is saying is: grass is not boring at all. I made this picture to show you how interesting grass can be. And it's not just grass. Lots of ordinary things become more interesting if you use art to help you look closely at them.

Albrecht Dürer, *Great Piece of Turf*, 1503

Imagine you've got a bike. It was fun at first, but now it feels pretty boring. One day an artist called Pablo Picasso was looking at his old bike. He was fed up with it. So he imagined it in a very different way. Picasso imagined it like this:

Pablo Picasso, *Tête de taureau (Bull's Head), bicycle seat and handlebars*, 1942

The next time Picasso went on his bike, he imagined he was riding on the back of a bull.

Picasso was one of the most famous artists of the 20th century. He was born in Spain but lived a lot of his life in Paris. He was very imaginative and kept changing his styles of drawing and painting.

So here's a big idea: it's not really things that are boring. It is just that sometimes our brains forget how to make them interesting. We can use art as a tool to help our brains find new ways of making ordinary things feel more exciting.

Now let's move onto another one of our big ideas around appreciation: *the importance of drawing.*

For most of history, there were hardly any pictures of anything. Every picture had to be made by someone, by hand – either being drawn or painted or sculpted. Only a few people ever saw a picture of themselves. Then, in the 1800s, photography was invented. But even after that, there weren't many pictures, because it was really complicated and expensive to take a photo. It was only for very special occasions.

Then, around the 1960s, smaller cameras were invented. They were still pretty complicated, though, with lots of switches and dials. And you couldn't see the photos until they'd been developed in a special shop. So if you'd been alive then and your mum took a photo of you playing on the beach on holiday you wouldn't get to see it until you got home.

It's only very recently (in the long story of history) that taking a photo has become incredibly quick and easy. Phones let us take pictures of anything, at any moment – which is amazing. But it's also a bit of a problem. When you can take photos of anything you want, whenever you want, you might not always look at things very carefully, because you know the camera will do the noticing for you. Let's see how this works. Suppose you see an interesting tree. You might take a photo of it, like this one:

A tree in the Karwendel area of the Austrian alps

Now we've got a challenge for you. In the box below, or on a sheet of paper, try to do a drawing from memory of the tree. Don't look back at the photo – just have a go.

It's hard, isn't it? When you've finished, compare your drawing to the photo. Did you notice that the tree splits about halfway up the trunk, and then the left-hand part splits into three big sections but the right-hand part splits into two? Did you include the green and white moss growing up the trunk? There are bound to be lots and lots of details that are different. Don't worry, it's not a test. It's just an experiment.

This experiment is telling us something important: most of the time, we do not look very carefully at things. But when you do a drawing of something, it's the opposite. Drawing makes you slow down and notice things your phone would never teach you to see. You have to look at it very carefully. Imagine you are drawing these leaves:

You have to notice lots of details. Obviously, the leaves are green, but are they all exactly the same shade? The edges are made up of little curvy bits, but each curve is different, and one is actually quite pointy. Each leaf has dark little 'veins' down the middle, but each of these is individual too, like a fingerprint.

One of the first people to recognise how important drawing is was a 19th-century English writer called John Ruskin. This is his drawing of an old, withered leaf:

John Ruskin, *Study of Spray of Dead Oak Leaves*, 1879

Ruskin liked to look closely at objects in nature. When he was little, he was lonely and didn't have many friends. His parents had a big garden, and he loved looking carefully at the plants. In the evening his father would read to him, and while he was listening, John would draw pictures. Sometimes he drew imaginary pictures of castles, but sometimes he'd draw whatever was around him.

Ruskin thought that everyone would be better if they spent more time drawing. He didn't think you needed to be very good at it. The important thing is that drawing makes you look very carefully at the world. When you've got your drawing-brain switched on, you notice much more of the world – and that makes everything more interesting.

What if you did a drawing of the kitchen table, or a car, or someone playing football, or even your own face (looking in a mirror, of course)? You might realise that you'd never really looked at any of these things carefully before.

Here is another idea to consider: art can help us love people. We want to love other people – our friends and family – but it's tricky because other people aren't nice all the time and lots of things can go wrong: maybe there's a disagreement or they get in a bad mood (or maybe you do).

Art can help us cope with the ups and downs of getting on with the most important people in our lives. Looking at art can help us understand people better (even when that feels hard).

The nice thing about these Russian dolls – called *matryoshka* dolls – is that they fit inside one another. The little ones are hidden inside the bigger ones. You might be looking at a big one, but you know the little ones (all the way down to the tiny baby doll) are still there inside. (They look old-fashioned, but they were only invented about a hundred years ago.)

It's the same with people. Mum or Dad are obviously 'big', but what's much less obvious is that there's a baby version of them, and a 5-year-old version, and a teenage version still there inside them.

That's why adults can be so surprising. They can seem very sensible most of the time, and then they suddenly panic or get upset or lose their temper. It's confusing. But maybe it's not so confusing if you think about the Russian dolls. When they get upset, it might just be the baby or 5-year-old or teenage version of themselves that's bothered.

Gerhard Altzenbach, *The Eleven Ages of Man*, 1609–1672

Artists have made pictures of this idea as well. They've tried to show how a person changes throughout their whole life – and how every earlier version of them is still part of who they are. Here's one that shows a person at every stage of life, from childhood to old age.

They're wearing old-fashioned clothes because this engraving was made a very long time ago, in the 17th century. 'Engraving' is a way of making many copies of the same picture. First you make the drawing by cutting grooves into a metal plate. Then you put ink into the grooves. When you press a piece of paper against the plate, the ink transfers onto the paper to make the image. You can repeat this again and again to make more copies.

We often forget that big people used to be little, and that little people will one day be big, and eventually old. Pictures like this help us imagine all the different 'versions' of a person at once – just like the Russian dolls – so we can appreciate people more and understand that everyone is still growing and changing.

In the 1600s there was a successful artist called Rembrandt. Starting in his twenties, he painted pictures of himself as he got older:

IN HIS TWENTIES

Rembrandt, *Self-Portrait*, c. 1629

IN HIS THIRTIES

Rembrandt, *Self-Portrait in a Flat Cap*, 1642

Rembrandt was the most famous artist of the 17th century. He was really good at using shadows; he made the light fall just on a few details so you would look at them very carefully, while other details were only half-seen. He loved eating huge meals and going to parties. He was very close to his son, Titus, who became an art dealer when he grew up.

It's very strange to see different pictures of the same person at different stages of their life all at the same time. Why is that?

When you look at Rembrandt's self-portraits, you might notice how much he changes. When he is young, he looks smooth-faced and serious; later he looks more confident; and in the last portrait his face is older, but also more interesting – full of lines and shadows that show he has lived a long and complicated life. His clothes are richer, and he looks calm and thoughtful as he paints.

IN HIS FORTIES

Rembrandt, *Self-Portrait*, 1652

IN HIS FIFTIES

Rembrandt, *Self-Portrait with Two Circles*, c. 1665–1669

When he was young, he didn't know how his life would go. He didn't know what successes and failures he would have. He didn't know what he would be like when he got older. But all these different selves are part of his story; it all happened.

Thinking about someone over their whole life doesn't necessarily make them easier to love, but it can make them easier to understand. Every person, at every age, has their own worries, hopes and stories. Everyone's life is so strange. When we see someone's whole journey, it can help us appreciate who they are and what they've been through. This leads us to our next big idea: art helps us see what's nice about people.

Some people look pretty interesting, like movie stars and pop singers. But most of us look quite normal. If people got to know us, they would realise how fascinating and special we are – it's just that, mostly, we look pretty ordinary. (It's a funny thing that 'ordinary' sounds like a bad thing, but actually, of course, nearly everyone is ordinary.)

A wonderful thing that some artists have done is to give their full, caring attention to someone who might seem ordinary to everyone else. And quite often the person they chose was their mother. Perhaps you can guess why: your mum might not look unusual to strangers, but to *you*, she is one of the most important people in the world.

Here's one artist who painted a picture of his mum. If you just glanced at her you might not think she was all that nice. She looks quite serious. James Abbott McNeill Whistler was an American artist, born in 1834. The painting is often called *Whistler's Mother*, but its real title – *Arrangement in Grey and Black No. 1* – shows that Whistler was thinking carefully about shapes and colours as well as about his mother.

James Abbott McNeill Whistler, *Arrangement in Grey and Black No. 1*, 1871

In this picture, Whistler is saying something quiet but powerful: 'My mum matters.' She looks very strict, but we also get the feeling that she was very calm, patient and loving. When her son said he wanted to be an artist she helped and encouraged him a lot. When he made friends she thought were a bit odd, she invited them to parties so she could get to know them properly – and ended up liking them too.

She's not laughing in the picture – she's just sitting quietly, being herself – but Whistler knew she had a very lovely smile. He wanted us to look at her with the same care and affection that he felt. You don't know what she's thinking exactly, but it feels like she's thinking about taking care of you. She's seen with love.

The artist is asking us to look as carefully as he looked. He knows his mother is really lovely, and he wants us to see that too. Loving someone means noticing the good things about them that aren't so obvious to other people. That's what this painting helps us practise. You could do the same with someone's dad or granny or little sister or cousin. And if you can do that, it means you can start to do it with almost anyone.

Detail from: Ludolf Bakhuysen, *Warships in a Heavy Storm*, c. 1695

Sometimes it can be helpful to look at art when you are having a hard time with someone you care about. Maybe you've had an argument, or someone snapped at you, or everything suddenly feels stormy inside your mind. Art can give you a picture of what those feelings are like and remind you that they usually pass.

In this picture the sea looks terrible. If you were on that ship, you would likely be in a huge panic – you'd think it was going to sink at any moment.

This picture was painted at the end of the 1600s in the Netherlands. The Netherlands had lots of very good sailors, and lots of good artists. It was one of the first countries where ordinary people – not just kings or very rich nobles – could buy paintings to decorate their homes. And they loved pictures of the things that mattered in their everyday lives – cooking, sitting with their friends, cleaning and, of course, ships. Sailing was a big part of Dutch life because a lot of their businesses depended on trade with other countries. And storms were something people knew well.

But the point is: even though the storm looks terrifying, this kind of ship has been through many storms before. The experienced sailors don't like storms, but they know they can get through them quite safely, and eventually the bad weather will pass. There is even a patch of blue sky in the distance if you look closely.

It's the same with feelings. Sometimes you're annoyed with your parents, or a friend at school says something unkind, and everything suddenly feels wild and out of control – almost like being on that ship. But the picture is saying: 'It looks terrifying out there, but actually the ship is going to be fine (and you'll be fine, too).'

This might not seem like it has anything to do with love, but it does. This is because art can help you with the ups and downs of your feelings about the people in your life.

Just as the sea is usually calm but sometimes there is a storm and it is full of frightening waves, our feelings about people can change from calm to stormy very quickly. When you're upset or overwhelmed, you might panic and think, 'Everything is ruined!' But this picture is telling us that actually, we can cope. It might be tricky for a while, but it's not really a disaster. Your mum or your dad or friend will calm down soon, and so will you. And you will feel close to that person again.

Art like this teaches appreciation in a different way: it helps you notice that a bad moment is only one part of a relationship, and reminds you to value the person – and your connection with them – even when your feelings are in a storm.

This is a picture that the artist Angelica Kauffman painted of herself (in a white dress) beside a figure who represents Poetry. The leaves in the other figure's hair aren't from real life – they're a symbol that she stands for poetry and imagination. The picture isn't just showing two friends having a chat; it's showing an idea: that different kinds of creativity can work together. The picture is about why two people are friends. They're different, but they help each other.

Angelica Kauffmann, *The Artist in the Character of Design, Listening to the Inspiration of Poetry*, 1782

Kauffman was a very successful artist. She was born in Switzerland but moved to London and Rome because there were opportunities for selling her paintings there. She had lots of interesting friends – including writers – and she liked painting pictures inspired by the things they talked about.

In this picture, the artist is listening carefully to Poetry. It's a reminder that you don't have to do everything alone. A friend doesn't need to be the same as you to help you grow. They can be a good friend because they're better than you at some things, and you might be better than them at others. Instead of being envious, you can get your friend to help you with things you aren't as good at. Together you make each other stronger. That's a big idea: appreciate your friendships and love your friends as best you can.

Art can also remind us about the places we live in, and what they are really like. When people want to say what's nice about the place where they live, they usually talk about the things that are obviously attractive. Suppose you lived in the Netherlands; you might show someone a postcard like this and say, 'This is what's great about living here.'

It is rather lovely. The problem is, it's hardly ever like this. In the picture, it's a sunny day, but actually there aren't many sunny days in the Netherlands. There's a nice boat going past, but mostly the boats on the rivers look quite different – they're usually carrying coal or scrap iron. The windmill looks as if people take care of it, but they're often neglected. If you went to the Netherlands expecting it to be like this, you'd probably be disappointed.

Some artists think differently. Instead of showing the very nicest things about a place, they concentrate on showing how a place can be lovely in ways you wouldn't usually expect.

As you'll see in the painting on the next page, it's not a very nice day; the banks of the river are messy and neglected and there's no pretty boat to take you on a trip. But the artist, Jacob van Ruisdael, still really loves this place. He likes seeing the shadows of the clouds on the water; he likes feeling cosy inside while it is grey and cold outside; and he likes the interesting old wooden posts that prop up the bank. He likes the weeds, and how a ray of sunlight is striking the side of the windmill, and he likes the shapes of the clouds too. Once they are pointed out, you might like these things as well.

Jacob van Ruisdael, *The Windmill at Wijk bij Duurstede*, c. 1668–1670

Van Ruisdael was born in Haarlem, in the Netherlands, in 1629. His father, uncles and brothers were all painters. In those days, being a painter was a family business. It was a skill you learnt, like being a plumber or a dentist. Nobody asked if you had a special talent or if it was right for you – they just thought it was a job like any other. Jacob liked painting clouds and water, so would often put the horizon low down in the picture (in this one, about two-thirds of the painting is just the sky).

There's a big point being made here. Often we get disappointed because we're looking for the obviously nice things, while actually there might be a lot of good things around – we just don't know how to see them.

A useful thing art can do is teach us to look in unexpected places for what we might like. The secret of appreciation is seeing the nice things about a place or a person that aren't immediately obvious. It's how we want other people to see us, and it's how – ideally – we should see them.

CHAPTER THREE

Hope

Sometimes it's hard to stay cheerful. It's not that anything awful or very sad has happened; we just feel glum. Imagine that the weather has been cold and wet for ages, and you've got lots of homework to do for school, or maybe your best friend is away on holiday and you're stuck at home. It's not surprising if you feel pretty gloomy.

This is one of the times when you need art – because quite a lot of art has been made specifically to cheer people up. Art is a tool for storing hopeful feelings and giving them back when we're feeling low.

One of the ways artists do this is by painting sunny pictures that make us feel better. This picture was painted in the early 19th century by Franz Ludwig Catel. It shows something that today feels ordinary but was still unusual at the time: someone on holiday. There were no cars, trains or planes so most people just stayed at home. But a few people did travel for pleasure and often they went to a city in Italy called Naples, because it was warm and got lots of sunshine. In the distance you can see the island of Capri, where, in ancient times, Roman emperors took their holidays.

The man in the painting is Karl Friedrich Schinkel, a famous architect who lived and worked in Berlin, Germany. In Berlin, the winter lasts for months and months and the sky is usually grey. Often it was freezing, and

Franz Ludwig Catel, *Schinkel in Naples*, 1824

Schinkel had to wear a huge, heavy coat. It was dark when he went to work and dark when he came home. He was extremely busy and hardly ever got a break to go somewhere warm.

But one time he did. He stayed in sunny Naples, where he could open the windows and look out across the trees to the sparkling water. There was the lovely island of Capri in the distance (you could take a boat there), the sky was blue, and in the evening he could have dinner outside and look up at the stars. He asked a friend to paint a picture of this so he could take it home with him. He put it on the wall of his room back in cold, dark Berlin, and every time he looked at it, it cheered him up.

Art can bottle happiness. We don't think about it much these days, but in the past 'bottling' was a hugely important human discovery. It's a way of preserving fruits and vegetables. You used to only get strawberries for a few weeks of the year, when they were ripe in the local fields and gardens – there was no way of keeping them fresh. You couldn't transport them from another country; it would have taken weeks on ships and they'd rot. They couldn't be grown in greenhouses either, because people didn't know how to make big, clear panes of glass yet. It was a pity, because a lot of people loved the taste of strawberries.

But then someone found out how to preserve strawberries. They cooked them and stored them in a jar or a bottle with a tight lid. And then they could open the jars in the middle of winter and have a taste of strawberries. It cheered them up.

Art does the same thing. It 'bottles' happy times – preserving them so we can have access to them when things aren't as nice.

Paolo Uccello, *The Battle of San Romano*, c. 1397–1475

These two paintings are called 'Renaissance' paintings. The Renaissance was an important change in thinking that began in Italy and then spread across Europe from about 1400.

Renaissance means 'rebirth' in Old French – and it was called this because people at the time felt they were rediscovering very old ideas from the Greeks and Romans. They thought these ideas were much better than the ones people were using at the time. They believed that progress didn't come from throwing away what had gone before, but from learning from the best parts of it.

In the 1400s, when these pictures were painted, there were lots of battles in Europe. It was horrible. There would be shouting and fighting, everyone

Detail from: Painter of central Italy (formerly Attributed to Luciano Laurana, c. 1420–1479), *View of an Ideal City*, or *The City of God*, c. 1470

would be in a panic, and it would all be very chaotic and frightening. So during this difficult time, artists liked to 'bottle' the special moments when everything was calm and peaceful – like early morning in a lovely city when there's no one around.

Of course, the past they were remembering wasn't perfect either – ancient Rome and Greece had their own problems and dangers. But the artists weren't trying to say those times were perfect. They were saying that even in troubled times, there are ideas and moments from the past that can give us hope and help us imagine a better future.

Another thing about the past was that it was not very easy for people to spend time alone. You can see what it might have been like in the following painting, *Gossip in the Salon*. You'd always be surrounded by people who were watching you or gossiping about you or asking you to do things or telling you long, boring stories about how their cousin's neighbour twisted their ankle.

Carl Schweninger the Younger, *Gossip in the Salon*, c. 1903

Unless you were quite rich, it was unusual to have a room of your own – like the woman in the next painting. The artist, Georg Friedrich Kersting, lived in Germany in the 19th century. He belonged to a movement in art called 'Biedermeier'. Biedermeier artists liked painting scenes of home life, and they loved quiet moments and tidy rooms. They were excited by questions like: How does ordinary life go well? What makes people happy?

You can understand how nice it must've been to be alone, to concentrate on what you wanted to do; to get on with your projects and interests and to have your mind to yourself. This picture bottled a rare, lovely moment of being alone. There is nothing you have to do – but you're not bored. There's so much you want to do on your own, and there's plenty of time.

Detail from: Georg Friedrich Kersting, *Embroiderer*, 1817

It's the people in this picture's day off. They're having a party with their friends down by the river.

Pierre-Auguste Renoir, *Luncheon of the Boating Party*, 1880–1881

Everyone is happy and the little dog is being sweet. Maybe they will go swimming later or start dancing. The artist made this picture to bottle this cheerful day. Most of the time these people had ordinary, busy lives – they worked hard, had chores to do and didn't often get long afternoons to relax. But this picture reminds them (and us) that soon it will be the weekend, and eventually it will be summer. There are days when everything feels fun and easy, and those days always come back again.

Pierre-Auguste Renoir was an Impressionist. That means he tried to capture the feeling of a moment. An odd thing about being human is that all our experiences only last a few seconds while they are actually happening. We look up and see people sitting around the table; a moment later they've all moved. But some moments are really lovely, and the Impressionists tried to capture with paint the happiest minutes of life.

Happiness is still there, in the picture. So much of the time we're in a rush – we have school, homework, activities, family plans and a hundred things to think about. It feels like life is always busy. So it's good to bottle times when we feel still, calm and happy in ourselves.

At those times we might feel a bit like the sculpture below. It was made in 1946 by Barbara Hepworth. The shape twists gently inwards, almost like a wave curling or a shell forming. It's so balanced, solid and clean. The smooth brown wood on the outside and crisp, white interior make it feel peaceful. It's not trying to do anything, it's just happy being itself and inviting a moment of calm.

Barbara Hepworth was one of the first women in England to become famous as an artist because, unfairly, for a long time it was mostly men who were allowed to have careers in art.

Barbara Hepworth, *Pelagos*, 1946

For much of her life, Hepworth lived in a town called St Ives, in Cornwall, on the far west tip of England. Following her example, lots of other artists moved to the same village. It must have been amazing to live there: being an artist would have felt quite normal rather than a bit unusual.

Works of art like these can help to remind us of our own tranquil moments. Bottling happiness is so important because life is full of ups and downs. When things are going badly, we lose touch with what's nice. We only think about what's awful and we feel that life is totally grim.

But that's not really fair – it's not that life is always bad, it's just that we're forgetting the lovely bits. When art bottles nice times and nice feelings, it means we can get hold of them when things aren't so good. And when we look at the images it brings back good feelings – just like when bottling was invented, it meant people could taste the lovely sweetness of a strawberry, even in the middle of winter.

Vincent van Gogh, *Roses*, 1890

Some people think that happy or bright pictures can be a bit babyish. They imagine that if you like a cheerful picture that feels warm or hopeful, it must mean you don't understand how difficult the world can really be. They think that 'serious' art should always look sad or gloomy.

But actually, the truth is that many artists who painted some of the most hopeful and uplifting pictures understood all about how hard and difficult life can be. All through his life, Vincent van Gogh painted lovely, cheerful pictures of flowers such as the roses on the previous page.

We saw a picture of van Gogh's bedroom on page 32. Van Gogh was born in the Netherlands in 1853 into quite a wealthy family. He was a serious and thoughtful child and he cared a lot about people who didn't have very much money. His brother Theo was his best friend. Amazingly, during his lifetime, hardly anyone wanted to buy his paintings, even though today any picture by him is worth an absolute fortune.

Van Gogh also had times when he felt very unwell and struggled with difficult thoughts and feelings. The self-portrait with a bandage on the next page shows one of those moments.

Even when he was having a hard time, he kept trying to paint things that felt nice, beautiful and hopeful. He knew how bad things can be. Painting cheerful things wasn't pretending that everything was fine; it was one of the ways he tried to remind himself that the world could still contain moments of colour and calm.

This is because our minds can do a very peculiar – and very fortunate – thing. Looking at something hopeful or cheerful can actually make us more able to cope with difficulties. Normally we suppose we'll only feel cheerful once our problems are solved. But actually, if we can lift our mood even a little, we often find we have more strength and are much better at solving our problems or dealing with whatever is going wrong. A small touch of brightness can help us keep going until things get better.

Vincent van Gogh, *Self-Portrait with Bandaged Ear*, 1889

CHAPTER FOUR

SADNESS

CHAPTER FOUR

Sadness

Sometimes you feel rather sad – and that's completely normal. Maybe a friend wasn't nice to you; you wanted to get onto the swimming team but you weren't picked; perhaps your family is going through a difficult time; someone said something mean to you at school; or you saw something upsetting on the news. There are lots of big and small reasons we can feel sad.

When you're feeling sad or upset, people usually try to cheer you up. They tell you that things are going to be OK, and that you will feel better tomorrow. They mean well, but actually they're not helping very much. You can get the impression that you are never supposed to feel sad – that if you are unhappy or a bit miserable or feel like crying, then there is something wrong with you.

But art is different. Art shows us that it is OK to be sad. Art is a tool for helping us cope with sadness.

A lot of artists have been intrigued by sadness. They see it as an important part of life that needs to be taken seriously. One way art can help with sadness is by being quite honest and admitting that things really can be a bit awful. It recognises that sometimes you *should* feel sad: it is a sensible, reasonable and completely natural thing to feel.

On the next page is an artist, Nicolas Poussin, who lived a long time ago. Sometimes he felt very sad. Poussin was born in 1594 in France. He wanted to be a painter, but in those days, painting wasn't considered a proper job for someone like him, so he ran away from home. For a while he had very little money and struggled to find work. After a while, things worked out and he became a great artist – but he never forgot how hard life can be.

Poussin did this drawing of himself while looking in the mirror. He was not feeling happy that day. His face looks tired and serious – he's showing us that people, even famous artists, can have sad and difficult moments.

Nicolas Poussin, *Self-Portrait*, c. 1630

This is another picture Poussin painted. It shows a terrifying moment: you are happily going through life in your little boat, and suddenly there's a terrible storm – the wind is blowing, the rain is lashing down and your boat is about to sink; the best you can hope for is that you might be able to cling to a rock ... but there's a snake slithering on the rocks nearby. Everything feels out of control.

Nicolas Poussin, *Winter or The Flood*, c. 1660–1664

This painting shows a scene from a story in the Old Testament, the first book of the Bible. In the story, God gets so angry that he sends a great flood to destroy everything on Earth. Most people weren't that bad, but their world collapsed.

Poussin wasn't painting it to frighten people; he was using the story as a symbol. He thought life can feel like this sometimes: one moment things seem normal, and then something unexpected happens and all the things you took for granted are washed away. Even if you haven't done anything terribly wrong, it can feel as though the whole world is against you.

These (hopefully) aren't exactly your problems. But if you told this painting all about your own sorrows it would say: *I know, I know, that's so hard, we can be sad together.* Art can sit with us in our sadness and help us see that feeling upset is a real and human thing. Sometimes we don't actually need to be cheered up at all – we need someone to understand and to agree that lots of things are unfair and disappointing and really very sad.

Perhaps that 'someone' who understands you is your teddy bear. Some people think teddy bears are just for children, and older kids sometimes feel like they're getting too old for a teddy. But that's not really true. In an important way, you will need a teddy bear all your life. You never grow out of needing something that helps you feel less alone when you're sad.

Boris Kustodiev, *Boy with Teddy Bear*, 1907

Let's think about what a teddy bear really is. It's got furry ears, a tiny pointy nose and a sweet little smile. That's very nice, but these are not the most important things about a teddy bear.

The really important thing is when you feel sad or lonely or lost, a teddy bear will be there with you. It doesn't ask you annoying questions, or tell you to cheer up, or say something is your fault. If you cry, it won't mind. It doesn't say anything at all, but somehow you know it understands. It stops you feeling so lonely. (You might get the same feeling from a knitted rabbit, a special blanket you rub against your nose or anything that has kept you company for a long time.)

No matter how young or old you are, there will always be times when you feel a bit sad or lonely or lost. This happens to everyone: it's part of being human. Our society hasn't been very good at making teddy bears for adults, but there's one place where grown-ups can find something very like a teddy bear – in art.

Take the next painting, for example. It isn't cuddly at all. But, like a teddy bear, it understands when you feel sad. It shows a very lonely, frozen place far out in the Arctic Sea. You can see that the ice sheets in the picture have been grinding against each other, pushing up jagged spikes.

Caspar David Friedrich, *The Sea of Ice*, 1823–1824

This picture knows all about feeling like there's too much pressure, or that everything is uncomfortable and difficult. It was painted by Caspar David Friedrich (you saw another of his works on page 56).

He was what we call a 'Romantic' painter. It doesn't mean he went on lots of dates! In art, the word 'Romantic' means an artist who thinks that nature is sending us messages if we look carefully, and that if we look at nature through the eyes of an artist, we can find comfort. Friedrich understood sadness well. When he was a boy, his younger brother fell through some ice and drowned, and the shock of it stayed with him all his life. Years later, some people think he painted this picture partly to express that old, painful memory.

If a picture could cry, maybe this one would. It's silently saying a really important thing that we sometimes need to hear: *I know how you feel. I feel the same. I'm here with you.*

This piece of sculpture, made by an artist named Richard Serra, is huge and impressive. It isn't hiding away. It doesn't try to be pretty or comforting.

Richard Serra was born in San Francisco in 1938. He lived in New York when he was older. He became famous for making ginormous, heavy sculptures out of metal and stone. When you stand near them, you notice how solid the sculpture is and you might feel very small and weak. You couldn't possibly knock over this enormous slab of stone or even move it an inch.

The sculpture is named after a poet called Fernando Pessoa, who lived in Portugal in the early 20th century. He wrote some beautiful and sorrowful lines, such as:

I know, I alone
How much it hurts, this heart.

And …

Richard Serra, *Fernando Pessoa*, 2007–2008

O salty sea, so much of whose salt
Is Portugal's tears!

Naming this sculpture after Pessoa invites us to think about serious feelings – like sadness and loneliness. The sculpture feels strong enough to hold those feelings without collapsing or apologising for them. So this work of art isn't just saying that it's OK to feel sad. It's saying something bigger: that sadness is an important part of being human, and sometimes it's important to feel sad.

Feeling sad doesn't mean there is something wrong with you. It doesn't mean you are weak, ungrateful or failing. It simply means you are paying attention to life – and life can be difficult. This art is telling us that clever, sensitive and good people feel like this sometimes.

This leads us to another big idea: art can be a tool to understand sadness, and it can also help us recognise companionship. Artists in the past often imagined that if you were feeling lonely and lost, another presence – a special friend, companion, or even a work of art – might come along and share the feeling.

The picture on the next page is telling us a story from long ago. A boy (he's the one wearing red trousers) is having a very hard time. His father isn't well, and the boy has to go on a long, difficult journey to get the right medicine. Along the way, he gets lost and becomes scared.

The artist imagines the ideal friend who can help him: an angel, with coloured wings and a little gold circle above their head to show that they are very kind. The angel understands how difficult it is, and they say encouraging things to the boy.

The angel says, 'I'll be friends with you because I can see you are feeling troubled, upset and sad.' Sometimes we think that being friends is only about having fun together, but a really important part of being friends is that we can feel sad together.

This picture was painted in Italy in the 1400s. It came from the workshop of Andrea del Verrocchio. He's not that well-known, but he was a really good teacher. He had an art school, and a lot of his pupils went on to become famous artists – including Leonardo da Vinci.

Workshop of Andrea del Verrocchio, *Tobias and the Angel*, 1470–1475

In your room, you have the modern versions of angels. They might not have wings or golden halos, but they do something very similar. You have your collection of things that can understand you and comfort you. You can keep them close to you, and they can be your companion. You won't have to face the tricky parts of every day alone, because these works of art are with you, by your side.

CHAPTER FIVE

BALANCE

Balance

We've looked at ways that art can be a tool for remembering, appreciation, hope and sadness. This next part of the book is about the idea of balance, and how art can help us with it.

'Balance' is a very interesting idea, but it's not really something people talk about a lot. You probably don't go around saying: *Oh, I wish I had more balance in my life!* Or: *I wish I could find some art to help me feel more balanced!* (Though you might after reading this chapter!) Often, we look to art because it reflects our lives, our feelings or our surroundings. But at other times, we want art to do the opposite. We want it to show us something that is missing from our lives – something we need more of. That is what we mean by balance here.

In order to introduce you to the idea of balance, let's look at a story about some things that happened a long time ago, between about 1800 and 1900. At that time, there was a big change happening in many countries. It was called the Industrial Revolution. What that means is that lots of new machines were being invented, huge factories were being built, the first railways were being made and there were many new roads, bridges and houses.

Large numbers of people moved from the countryside to work in factories and towns. Cities grew much, much bigger very quickly. Before this, most people lived on farms or in little villages. But now, nearly everyone was living in towns and cities, on crowded streets with rows and rows of houses, hardly any trees, and often not even a garden to sit in. Mostly people earned more money than before, because you could get paid more for working in a factory than for working on a farm – so it wasn't all bad – but it was a big change to how people lived.

What kind of art do you think became popular during the Industrial Revolution? You might expect people to want pictures of the new factories and busy streets, or steam trains racing through tunnels. But that's not what happened. Instead, this is the kind of art that became very popular:

Helen Allingham, *Old Cottages at Pinner*, 1885-1895

What people wanted were pictures of the things they missed: cottages, trees, flowers and quiet country lanes. They were looking for balance.

This is telling us something important. Art isn't only about showing us what life is like. Sometimes it shows us what life isn't like – and what we wish it could be like, at least for a while. Art is a tool for balance. It can give us the things that are missing from the rest of our lives. And by doing that, it can help us feel more complete.

We can use this idea of balance to help us make sense of something pretty puzzling: you will start to notice that people like very different things. For example, people have very different ideas about what makes a kitchen nice. For some people, this is what they'd like a kitchen to look like:

Why might that be? Probably because it looks relaxed and cosy – like it doesn't matter if you make a bit of a mess. That can be very appealing if you feel that in other parts of your life (at school or at work), you have to concentrate hard, try to get everything right and be on your best behaviour all the time. This kitchen balances the demanding, formal bits of life. If your dad likes this kitchen, it might be because he feels everyone is making too many demands on him (poor Dad!).

People like the things that are missing from their lives. They like the things that restore balance.

What if this is someone's perfect kitchen? Everything is under control, clean and beautifully organised. Why might someone really like that?

Imagine if the rest of their life was a bit chaotic: they are always in a rush, they have got a laptop in one hand, their car keys in another, they're trying to arrange a business meeting at the same time as checking Granny's OK and making sure their child is wearing a warm coat (it's a cold day) and they need to check there are enough eggs in the fridge to make an omelette. When everything else feels a bit chaotic, a space like this can feel soothing. This kitchen shows what's missing from their life – that's why they like it.

We can ask the same questions about works of art. First, ask yourself:

What do I notice here?
How does this picture make me feel?

Then you might wonder:

What kind of person might really like this picture?
What might they feel is missing in their life – calm, energy, order, freedom, quiet, excitement?

Detail from: Raffaello Sanzio, *The School of Athens*, 1509–1511

This fresco was done by Raffaello Sanzio, also known as Raphael. For a long time, people thought he was the best artist who ever lived (though not so many people feel this way today). The picture shows a selection of the cleverest people who had ever lived up to that point. They actually lived at different times and in different places, but Raphael visualized them all meeting up and talking together. Imagine hiding in the corner and listening to what they were saying.

Someone might love this picture because they care a lot about ideas. Suppose they feel that people do not pay enough attention to thinking carefully – they feel like everyone just chats about silly things all the time. This picture would be lovely for them because it shows everyone talking about important things, listening carefully and thinking deeply.

Someone else might be drawn to a very different kind of picture. Suppose a person feels that too many people are noisy or showing off and trying to be the centre of attention. They might really like a painting like the one on the next page because it's very quiet and calm. It's happy just to exist peacefully in the background and let you look slowly.

Giorgio Morandi was born in Bologna, Italy, in 1890 and he lived there his whole life. He didn't really care about selling his paintings. He just painted things that he liked and that meant a lot to him. To his surprise, he discovered that they meant a lot to other people as well.

Giorgio Morandi, *Still Life, Natura Morta*, 1953

What he loved most was going around his house and collecting jars and bottles that he liked, arranging them on a table, and spending hours just copying how the light and shadows fell on them.

People like different kinds of art because different things are missing in each person's life.

Now let's ask some quite personal questions:

What do you already have plenty of in your life?
What might you like a little more of in your life?

A good way to find out is to ask another question:

What do you enjoy looking at?

The kinds of pictures you're drawn to can give you clues about what helps you feel most like yourself. Suppose you like this:

A picture of a colony on Mars

It is pretty amazing to imagine a whole city living under a huge glass cover. There aren't any cities like that on Earth. There is a sense of adventure here: you're going to a new place.

Remember, we've been saying that we often like things because they give us something that's missing in our everyday lives. You might like an exciting picture about an unknown place because you feel like your life isn't exciting enough. The excitement in the picture perhaps makes up for the lack of excitement you normally feel. This can tell you something about what you enjoy in art. You might like art that's exciting and fantastical, that imagines new worlds and places.

Pieter Bruegel the Elder, *The Tower of Babel*, 1563

This picture is about people trying to build a tower so high that they'd be able to reach the sky. Of course, they didn't succeed – but it was a fantastic ambition. You can imagine them thinking that if only they could build a bit higher, they might finally find out what was up there.

Caspar David Friedrich, *Wanderer Above the Sea of Fog*, c.1817–1818

The story of people wanting to build towers to reach the sky is an old one. Before there were aeroplanes or telescopes, people didn't know how far away the sky actually was. It looks like it could be close, but actually the sky is made up of lots of layers of air and you can't touch it all. Building a tower isn't going to help. Beyond our atmosphere, there's nothing immediately exciting: just a few rocks, the odd satellite and miles of emptiness before you get to the Moon – but the wish to explore and understand the unknown is still very human.

Or if you like pictures about adventure, you might like this painting by Caspar David Friedrich. Unusually, we are seeing this character from behind, when most paintings show us people's faces. From this viewpoint, we can imagine it's us standing there on the craggy mountaintop, looking out over the mist into the distance. If you were in this picture, you could do whatever you want. No one is telling you what to do, and you don't have to fit in with other people. You can just go off on an adventure on your own.

Or maybe, instead of those things, you like looking at this:

It is a great picture. It shows someone who is powerful. They can do exciting things and make things happen: they can score a goal and lead their team to victory. That might appeal a lot, especially if, at the moment, you don't feel very powerful yourself; if you feel you can't influence things or make much happen. Your brain notices what feels missing and gets interested when it sees the missing quality reflected in a picture. You might feel something similar in a gallery when you look at this picture:

Jacques-Louis David, *Napoleon Crossing the Alps or Bonaparte at the St Bernard Pass*, c. 1800–1801

It also shows a powerful person – someone who can make things happen. He tells the whole army what to do and makes big decisions – he is a leader. He might win a big battle. This picture is by the French artist Jacques-Louis David. It's of his hero, the most ambitious political leader of the 19th century, Napoleon Bonaparte. When he was still in his twenties, Napoleon led his army across the Alps – something that many people at the time thought would be impossible. The artist has painted Napoleon confidently pointing the way forward, as if he were saying, 'Let's go right over the mountains!'

Ideas like these could be exciting if you spend a lot of your life at school and don't feel like you're in charge of much in your life. A picture like this offers a feeling of confidence and direction – even if real life doesn't always feel that way.

Or maybe you're not really into sports, power or discovering new worlds. Instead, you might be excited by this:

A Jaguar car

It feels very glamorous and elegant – and maybe your own life doesn't feel like that at all. You might be surprised to find that people felt something very similar thousands of years ago, when they made this sculpture:

Winged Victory or Nike of Samothrace, c. 200–190

This very old statue was made in ancient Greece, more than two thousand years ago. It used to have a head and arms, but they were broken off centuries ago. The figure is Nike, the Greek goddess of victory. You might already know her name from somewhere else. The sportswear brand Nike took their name from this goddess, and the swoosh logo was inspired by the goddess's wing.

It's a glamorous and elegant sculpture. There's a feeling of lightness and ease, of controlled strength, victory and triumph. It's not surprising that we get excited by flashy cars and grand statues. People long ago were just as excited by ideas of success and achievement as we are today.

Art can sometimes seem very different from the kinds of things you normally enjoy looking at. But actually, there's a secret connection. The things you are drawn to – whether it's sport, adventure or glamour – are often the things that bring balance to your life; they make up for what's missing. And it is the same with the right works of art. They give you feelings you might not get enough of day to day, helping you to feel a bit more complete just by being nearby.

NEW
NEW F
CHOOSE
OUR SHOES
MUSHROOM
Adventure!
OUT NOW!
NEW! BIGGER! BETTER!

CHAPTER SIX

MAKING SENSE OF MONEY

Making Sense of Money

When you were little, you probably didn't think about money very much. But as you grow up, you start to realise that money is one of the forces that shapes the adult world. Nearly all grown-ups think about money every day.

Money can be extremely useful. It helps builds schools and hospitals. It pays for buses and trains. It is why there are books, games, clothes, phones, food and other useful things in shops. It's why you can order a pizza, go on holiday, have a bath or watch a film. Without money moving around the world, a lot of everyday life wouldn't work.

But money can also be confusing. One problem starts with an obvious fact: lots of nice things are very expensive. When we think about these things, our brains can make an easy but unfortunate mistake. We start to think that *only* expensive things can be exciting or important – and that if something is cheap, then it must be boring or not very good.

When things are expensive, we tend to pay them a lot of attention. We notice what is impressive about them, because we think if something costs a lot then it must have a high value. And when something does not cost much, we often don't pay much attention.

Art can help us with this problem. That's because a lot of art is fascinated by things that don't cost very much – and pays them a lot of attention.

This isn't a fancy place to live at all. If the people who lived here had a lot of money, they might have paid someone to fix the pole holding up the climbing plant – or perhaps they'd just go and live in a bigger house in another part of the city.

Pieter de Hooch, *The Courtyard of a House in Delft*, 1658

But the artist liked this place exactly as it was – that's why he spent a long time painting a picture of it. He loved this little courtyard, with its funny little door in the wall. He liked the old wooden bucket and the broom used to brush the bricks every day. The family liked sitting out there on sunny days; perhaps it was where the little girl took her first steps not very long after her first birthday.

Pieter de Hooch, who painted this picture, was born in the Netherlands in 1629. His father was a bricklayer, which may help to explain why he painted every single brick in this courtyard so carefully. He was not a wealthy man, and he particularly loved painting pictures of people just doing ordinary things at home.

The artist of the next painting, Francisco de Zurbarán, was really excited by very ordinary kinds of fruit: just lemons and oranges, which don't cost very much at all. In his paintings, Zurbarán specialised in making objects stand out clearly against a dark background. His parents were poor, but eventually Francisco became the King of Spain's favourite painter.

Francisco de Zurbarán, *Still Life with Lemons, Oranges and a Rose*, 1633

Today, most people can buy fruit like this easily from a local shop – so we don't usually stop and think how lucky we are to have it.

But maybe we *should* stop and think – because an orange is actually an amazing thing. It smells fresh, it's tasty and it's good for you. It's just that we forget that it is amazing because it's familiar and affordable. When we look at a work of art like this, we start to remember. Art is showing us something important here: it helps us to love ordinary things.

If we only focus on expensive things, we are going to feel unhappy, because most of the time we can't afford them. But art reminds us that there are lots of wonderful things in the world that don't cost much at all – and that is very good news for our lives. In this way, art is like advertising for what we really need.

Let's think for a moment about something that might seem like the opposite of art: advertising. You've seen millions of adverts in your life – but what is an advert trying to do? Basically, an advert suggests that you should buy something to solve a problem. It might be saying:

Are you unhappy with your shoes?
Buy these shoes instead.

Are you worried about your hair?
Buy this special shampoo; it will make your hair look nice.

Are you bored?
Play this game.

You might think there are adverts for everything, but actually that isn't true. There are lots of important and wonderful things that normal advertising doesn't talk about at all.

Works of art are often a bit like adverts. They are trying to get you interested in something and show you how it could help you. But usually, the things artworks are trying to 'sell' you don't actually cost anything.

Christen Købke, *View of Østerbro from Dosseringen*, 1838

In the 19th century, a Danish artist called Christen Købke made lots of adverts for the sky.

Christen Købke was born in Denmark, and he started studying to be an artist when he was only twelve years old. He painted some very beautiful pictures, but he was not very successful at selling them during his lifetime. It is only quite recently that he's been properly appreciated as a painter.

You can't buy the sky, but Købke wanted you to notice it and be interested in looking at it. He thought that if we paid more attention to the sky, our lives would be better. Maybe he was right. When you look at the clouds in the sky, you often stop worrying so much about small problems – you feel a bit freer, at least for a little while.

This next painting is an advert for staring out of the window.

Gustave Caillebotte was born in Paris in 1848. He painted this picture in his own apartment in that same city. The man standing at the window is his younger brother, whom he was very fond of. Caillebotte studied law and engineering but later decided he wanted to be an artist. He enjoyed gardening and sailing, and was very good friends with Renoir, the painter we met earlier (see page 102).

Gustave Caillebotte, *Young Man at His Window*, 1875

It doesn't cost anything to stare out of the window. If you spent a lot of time staring out of the window at school, people might laugh or the teacher might tell you off – but this art-advert is saying that staring out of the window can be a very good thing, and you should give it a try. It helps you notice the world outside, and just as importantly, it gives you the chance to notice what's going on inside your own mind. Interesting, unusual and important thoughts start to emerge when you let yourself look and think.

Agnes Martin was born in Canada in 1912, but she lived most of her life in the United States. She enjoyed being alone and chose to live far away from big cities, in quiet places in the countryside. She even built herself a simple house made of mud. She made many pictures like the one on the next page, carefully drawing each line by hand.

Agnes Martin, *Wheat*, 1964

It is like an advert for being quiet. Normally, people who make a lot of noise get more attention. If you are quiet, people might think you are boring or that you don't have much to say. However, Martin's picture is saying that, actually, it's quite lovely to be quiet.

The picture might be telling you that you need more quietness in your life – and there are plenty of people who could benefit from 'buying' a little more quiet in their lives!

Buddhist Statue of Guanyin, Shanxi province, China, Jin dynasty, 1115–1234

This sculpture is an advert for listening. It was made in China nearly a thousand years ago. It represents a Buddhist figure called Guanyin, also known as the Goddess of Mercy. Guanyin was famous for her compassion. When someone was in trouble or feeling sad, she would listen to them and try to help them.

The statue seems to be saying: *You can bring me your worries and problems. I'll listen patiently and I won't jump to any conclusions. Tell me more. Let me know what is bothering you.* That feeling is very comforting. Being listened to properly can make a huge difference. When someone really listens, we feel less alone, and our problems often feel a little lighter. We really need to advertise listening: we need other people to hear what we have to say, and they need us to listen to them, too.

This is another way that art can help us. Ordinary advertising tries to persuade us to buy things. But works of art do something different. They are like adverts for good things that can happen inside our own heads, for free – things like how we feel about ourselves, how we feel about other people, and what we think is important and valuable. What's going on inside our heads and how we treat ourselves and other people makes a much bigger difference to our happiness, rather than what we buy.

Another tricky thing about money is how it is shared out. Some people have a lot of money and other people don't have very much at all. Often, our society pays a lot of attention to people who make a lot of money. We notice them, talk about them, and sometimes admire them – and sometimes they really are impressive.

But this can mean we don't always notice people who don't have much money. We might assume their lives aren't especially interesting and we don't often stop to admire them.

However, some art is very impressed by people who don't have a lot of money. The woman in this picture hasn't got much money. Her job is making lace. In the days when this picture was painted, you couldn't earn very much money making lace.

Not many people would have been interested in this woman at the time. They might have thought she wasn't worth paying attention to or was unimportant because she was poor. But the artist has a very different idea. He thinks she is wonderful. She has a kind, thoughtful face. She looks patient and gentle. She is skilful with her hands. She might be lovely to talk to, and she'd probably be a good friend.

Caspar Netscher, *The Lace Maker*, 1662

Caspar Netscher was originally going to be a doctor, but he was so good at drawing that his friends encouraged him to become an artist instead. He became successful, and kings and queens bought his paintings. Later in life he became ill and had to stay in bed, so he had his paints brought into his bedroom so he could continue working.

Have you ever seen someone asking for help in the street? It can feel quite upsetting. This painting shows an old man in exactly that position.

Jacques-Louis David, *Belisarius Begging for Alms*, 1781

The man with the white beard in this picture is Belisarius, a famous general from long ago. People at the time believed that he had once been powerful and admired but later lost everything and ended up dependent on others. In the painting, he's asking people to help him.

But let's take a closer look at him. The picture is in the 'classical' style, which means that the position of every detail is very carefully thought out. For instance, the old man's right hand is exactly in the centre of the image, so we are made to stop and really notice him.

The artist has also included an important detail: if you look carefully, you can see a little bit of his armour poking out from under his cloak on his shoulder. It's a clue to who he used to be.

The painting reminds us that a single moment doesn't tell us the whole story of a person's life. A very good person can end up in a very difficult situation. Someone who looks weak or unfortunate now may once have been strong, admired and confident. And someone who seems successful today could one day need help themselves.

Artists like David were interested in helping us look at people with more patience and respect. The picture is not suggesting that hardship is good; it is just saying that everyone has a story, and it's usually more complicated than it looks – and that's a very important concept.

BIG IDEAS FROM ART
ART!
ART.

ART IN YOUR LIFE

Art in Your Life

You've been trailing around the gallery for a while now and you've seen lots of pictures and sculptures. But before you leave the gallery, there is one last place you pass through: the gift shop. A lot of people think the gift shop is just there to make money for the gallery. But actually, it is asking one of the most important questions art can ask. The question is:

What do you want to take home with you?

A lot of the art probably didn't interest you much. But maybe there were one or two things that intrigued you – a picture you kept thinking about, or a feeling you didn't quite expect. So, how do you take those nice things back into your life? (We're not recommending coming back in the middle of the night with a van, climbing in a back window and carting off a couple of priceless masterpieces!)

If the gift shop could speak it would say something like this:

I'm glad you liked looking at a picture of some rocks in gallery XI at 3.14 p.m. today, and at the picture of clouds in the big room with the green walls at 3.57 p.m., but it might be years before you come back. It would be great if the things you've enjoyed in art could be part of your everyday life. What can I do to make that happen?

The shop is asking a great question, but mostly it is not very good at answering it. The shop might suggest you buy a mug – or maybe a tea towel – with the name of a famous artist on it. That could be quite fun. But it's not really helping you to take the experience you had when looking at the art home with you. It's not really the artist's name that matters, but what they were saying to you through their art – and the mug and the tea towel don't seem to know anything about that.

Actually, the most important things in the gift shop are the postcards on sale. Some people find that quite a surprising thing to say. A postcard is usually the cheapest thing in the shop, while the actual work itself might cost as much as ten or even a hundred houses. The original was carefully created by hand, by a genius with paints, brushes, pencils or clay, while the card was churned out by a machine in a factory.

But a postcard is a wonderful thing. You can hold it in your hand, you can press your nose up to it to look at a detail, or you can put it on the floor and lie down beside it – and the postcard is sending you exactly the same message as the real artwork when you saw it in the gallery.

Remember, we've been saying that works of art are always sending us messages. They might be saying:

An apple can be lovely.

Looking at the sky helps you calm down.

Someone who doesn't have much money might be fascinating.

But probably, the time when you most need to hear those messages is not when you are in the gallery. Galleries are really bad at timing. The artworks in them might be sending you messages that are really useful – but they are sending them at the wrong time.

Postcards solve this problem because you can keep them in your room, in your own private gallery, and they are around to help you whenever you need them.

Let's see how this works (to take just one example, though there are many) when you are feeling shy. It's not very nice feeling shy: you feel awkward, and you are worried that someone might ask you something that you don't know the answer to; or you feel you are supposed to say something, but you don't know what. Your skin gets very hot and you feel like you might cry.

Here's a postcard that could help. It's called a 'historical picture'. It shows an event from around 1600, a long time before it was painted, in 1817. The man on the left (the one wearing the orange tights) is a very important person – the Spanish ambassador. The Spanish ambassador had come there to meet an even more important person – the King of France, who normally looked like he does on the next page.

Jean-Auguste-Dominique Ingres, *Henry IV Receiving the Spanish Ambassador*, 1817

But the ambassador got a big surprise. Instead of striding around in his armour or sitting on a throne with his crown on, the king was crawling around the room pretending to be a horse, while his children were riding on his back. They were having a great time.

The artist, Jean-Auguste-Dominique Ingres, wanted to show that kings were real people as well. They too could feel sad, or stub their toe, or burp, or enjoy playing with their children. Ingres wanted to show that someone could be nice and kind as well as powerful and important.

Jacques Boulbene, Henry IV, *King of France and Navarre*, c. 1600

This is an important thing to think about, because often when we feel shy it's because we are only considering what the other person looks like just at that moment, and what they might think or say about us.

Maybe just now they look very imposing, or different to us, or clever or serious. But if we could see them at other moments in their lives, we'd realise they have lots of other more ordinary and human sides to them. They can be funny and silly, unsure of themselves and really quite a lot like us. If we remembered that, we wouldn't feel so worried about talking to them, and we wouldn't feel so shy.

This can sometimes happen if your mum or dad run into one of their friends when you are out, or if someone comes round for dinner. You look at this adult you don't know, and you can't think of anything to say.

If you often get shy, it can help to remember that shyness usually starts inside us and doesn't come from other people. You could try looking at a postcard of this picture and thinking about the ways that people who make you feel shy might have silly, ordinary sides to them too. The important thing is that the useful message a painting is sharing doesn't have to stay stuck in the gallery. You can take a postcard home and use it whenever you need it.

Now let's consider another big idea to do with art and objects: *how the things we own can help shape how we feel.*

Adults sometimes worry about something called being 'materialistic'. 'Materialistic' is quite an odd word, and maybe it's not one you've used much, but you probably know about the idea that it represents. Adults use it when they want to say that someone cares too much about physical things – like cars, houses, fancy watches or clothes – and not enough about their friends or being kind to people. They are too interested in their possessions and showing them off.

When people talk like this, it can sound as if caring about things is always a bad idea, and that if you are interested in material stuff then you can't also be interested in ideas, feelings, friendships or kindness. We could call these other things 'soul stuff'.

'Soul' is a useful word for talking about your sense of being you: your thoughts, feelings, ideas, hopes, worries, longings and memories; your experiences of love, happiness or sadness; your friendships and interests. All these things are inside you. Together, they make up your 'soul'.

But actually, there can be an overlap. Sometimes the *right* material things are closely connected to important soul stuff.

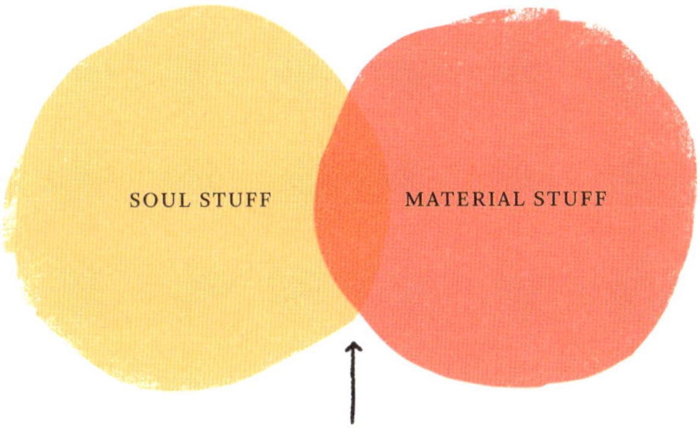

GOOD MATERIALISM

The overlap isn't an accident. It's there for a good reason: material things can help us with love, being nice, friendship and kindness.

Duncan Grant, *A Painted Pottery Dish*, c. 1930

Let's look at an example of how this can happen. This is a plate that belonged to some people living in England at the start of the 20th century. These people lived in the countryside and often had interesting friends to stay. They wrote books, painted pictures and had long conversations. They cared a lot about ideas, feelings and friendships – about 'soul stuff'.

On the next page is a picture of them. They were known as the 'Bloomsbury Set', a group of writers, artists and intellectuals who lived and worked together in the first half of the 20th century.

The Bloomsbury Set at Charleston farmhouse, in Sussex, England

Of course, they needed to have plates to put food on. Imagine putting a pile of spaghetti straight onto the table! But a plate can do more than just hold food. What else?

The plate looks cheerful. It's colourful, with lots of bright yellow – like sunshine – so if you're not in a very good mood when you sit down to dinner, it can cheer you up. It's a big plate, too. It isn't just for one person; rather it's for sharing food in the middle of the table – it's generous.

And look at the curved edge. Each curve flows into the next. There's lots of movement, but all the movement fits together. Imagine a conversation with someone that went like this: you say something (one curve), and they say something else (another curve), and the ideas meet nicely before moving on again.

It's an interesting thought: the shape of the plate is a bit like the shape of a good conversation. It's also a very personal plate. In the middle there is a picture of a basket of flowers. The flowers were collected from their garden, and the basket was a present from a friend.

It is a plate, but it's not just a plate. It's also talking to the people who use it about friendship, sharing, conversation and happiness. It is material stuff – but it is soul stuff too. You can understand why someone might want to buy a plate like this. It's a good possession to have. In a way it *is* materialistic to want to buy it – after all, the plate is 'stuff', just like a new pair of trainers or a TV.

But it's not the kind of materialism that's only about showing off or having lots of things you don't really need. It's something different. The plate isn't just there to impress people; it's there to *do a job*. It helps with sharing food, with conversation, and with creating a warm, friendly atmosphere.

Often people think art just means pictures and statues. But now we're seeing that a plate can be a work of art as well – not because it's in a museum, but because it does the same thing as other works of art:

Art is a tool for reminding us about soul stuff.

This isn't just a story about some people who lived a long time ago and owned a nice plate. It's also a story about you. Maybe you wouldn't want *that* exact plate. But one day you will buy some plates (practically every adult has to buy some plates at some point in their life). In fact, you'll be buying a lot of things.

This is the grown-up version of what we've been talking about all along: choosing what posters you'd like in your ideal room. Now we're imagining all the other things you might choose one day. But it's very much part of the same conversation because these other things can be art as well. What things would be in your ideal room?

'Good materialism' involves thinking carefully about ordinary possessions and asking what each one could *mean* to you – in the same way we've been asking what works of art might mean to you.

Let's think about chairs, for instance. If you don't want to sit on the floor, you're going to need a chair. But there are lots of kinds of chairs. So what sort of chair would you choose?

A chair can be a work of art. Like a painting or a sculpture, it can send you messages about what's important to you. And every chair sends a slightly different message. When you are choosing a chair, you are really trying to choose what message it would be good for you to hear, again and again.

The chair below, on the left, is talking about being alert and upright; you can't really slouch in it. It's straightforward. You can see exactly how it was made. It wants you to get organised and get some work done. Maybe that's the kind of encouragement you sometimes need.

The chair on the right is more interested in dignity and formality (it's a little bit like a throne). It says people should listen to what you say, which might be helpful if you sometimes feel hesitant about saying what you really believe.

Antique Windsor Chair, 18th century

French Wing Back Chair, 19th century

Here's a chair that's comfortable but very unfussy. It invites you to lean back, listen and think. It's saying: don't rush, get things clear in your own head before you act; don't worry too much about what other people think; make your own decisions.

Black leather armchair, 20th century

It doesn't need to be a chair; it could be something simple and inexpensive that carries a similar message. Forks can be art too.

Cutlery is another thing that you will definitely buy at some point in your life (though you might prefer to use chopsticks). This fork is very simple and efficient. It doesn't want to be complicated or fancy or make a fuss.

The next fork is rounded and elaborate. It likes making clear distinctions. Each part is separate, with the top coming to a definite end before the narrow middle section and finally the curved handle. It does not like muddling things up.

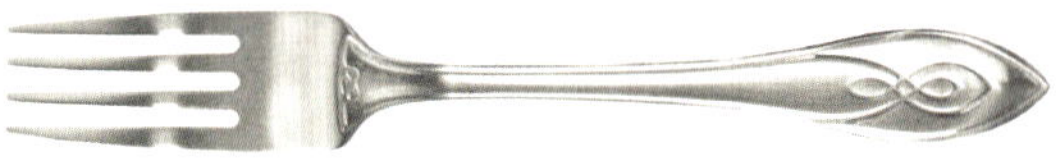

This fork is happy being unusual. It's decorative and doesn't mind being complicated.

Sometimes you might worry about standing out from the crowd, because it can feel lonely to be different. But this fork is saying something rather kind and useful: *Don't worry too much – I'm different too, and we can be different together.*

You can see how even something as ordinary as a fork can send us messages like a work of art. It has an opinion about what's nice or important. And just by choosing which fork you like, you can decide what kinds of messages you want to have in your life every time you eat your dinner.

Maybe it seems strange to be talking about chairs and forks in a book about art. But actually, it makes good sense. Art is any object that sends you an important, helpful message about your life.

Sometimes that message comes from a picture or a statue. But it could equally come from an 'ordinary' object, like a cup or a bag, a table or a spoon, sunglasses or an umbrella. What matters is that, across your life, you surround yourself with the images and objects that help you become the best version of yourself – even if that version looks quite different from anyone else's.

To speak very grandly for a moment, the aim of civilisation is that all the material, physical things we make, own or use – including works of art – should help our souls. They should encourage us to be kinder, more patient, more confident, more forgiving, more understanding of other people and of ourselves, calmer, clearer about what is really important to us, and better able to cope with the unavoidable difficulties of being alive.

The right images and objects can have a good influence on us – and that matters, because so often we don't feel kind or forgiving or patient or very good at coping. Art exists to help us at exactly those moments.

And finally ... A lot of adults think that art belongs mainly in art galleries and museums. That's understandable, because that's where many famous artworks are kept. But it can also be misleading. Art isn't only something to visit occasionally, behind glass and labels. It's something that can be part of everyday life.

What we are saying is that art doesn't really belong *only* in art galleries at all. It really belongs in your life – in your room, in your home, in the things you look at and live with. Art is important to you because it helps you.

It won't be all art that helps you – just some. You're starting out on a lifelong project to find the few works of art that matter most to you: the ones that comfort you, steady you, encourage you or help you understand yourself and other people a little better. Eventually you'll find the ones you need. And maybe, when you are older – in ten years' time or so – you will remember this book and feel that it helped you begin that search. That's what we hope.

What are YOUR Big Ideas?

p. 13 Andrea del Sarto, *Madonna of the Harpies*, 1517. Oil on canvas, 207 × 178 cm. Uffizi Gallery, Florence

p. 14 Constantin Brancusi, *Fish*, 1926. Bronze, metal and wood, 93 × 50 × 50 cm. Tate, London. Accepted by HM Government in lieu of tax and allocated to the Tate Gallery 1996. © 2026 Succession Brâncu. All rights reserved. ADAGP, Paris and DACS, London

p. 18 (top left) Pablo Picasso, 1965. TASS Archive/ Diomedia

p. 18 (top middle) Guillermo Kalho, *Frida Kahlo*, 1932. Gelatin silver print, 15.2 × 10.8 cm.

p. 18 (top right) Andy Warhol, detail from a photo of Jimmy Carter with Andy Warhol during a reception for inaugural portfolio artists, June 14, 1977. U.S. National Archives and Records Administration, ARC 175147

p. 18 (bottom left) Nadar, *Portrait of Claude Monet*, 1899.

p. 18 (bottom middle) Alfred Stieglitz, *Georgia O'Keeffe*, 1930. Gelatin silver print, 23.9 x 19.1 cm. Alfred Stieglitz Collection, National Gallery of Art, Washington, D. C.

p. 18 (bottom right) Yayoi Kusama stands in front of one of her paintings in her studio, Tokyo, Japan, on Wednesday, Oct. 18, 2006. Photo Jeremy Sutton-Hibbert /Alamy

p. 19 (left) Unknown artist, *Portrait of William Cullen (1710-1790)* (detail), 18th century. Oil on canvas. Private collection. Photo Fine Art Images/Diomedia

p. 19 (middle) *Portrait of Carl von Linde*. Edgar Fahs Smith Collection, Kislak Centre for Special Collections, Rare Books and Manuscripts, University of Pennsylvania

p. 19 (right) 'Lady Edison' with her latest invention: an air baby doll that can be bathed,1927. Photo Harris & Ewing. Library of Congress, Washington, D. C., Prints & Photographs Division, LC-H2- B-2330

p. 23 The Tribuna in the Uffizi gallery, Florence, Italy. Designed by Bernardo Buontalenti for Francesco I de' Medici, c.1580s. Photo B. O'Kane/Alamy

p. 25 The Breakfast Parlour, Sir John Soane's Museum, Lincoln's Inn Fields, London, c. 1813. © Richard Bryant/ Arcaid Images

p. 27 Anthony Van Dyck, *Charles I (1600–1649) with M. de St Antoine*, 1633. Oil on canvas, 370 × 270 cm. Royal Collection, London

p. 28 Titian, *Portrait of Clarissa Strozzi (1540–1581)*, 1542. Oil on canvas, 121.7 × 104.6 cm. Photo Artexplorer /Alamy

p. 29 Joseph Mallord William Turner, *Ulysses deriding Polyphemus*, 1829. Oil on canvas,132.5 × 203 cm. National Gallery, London

p. 31 Vincent van Gogh, *Eugène Boch*, 1888. Oil on canvas, 60.3 × 45.4 cm. Musée D'Orsay, Paris. Photo Peter Barritt/Alamy

p. 32 Vincent van Gogh, *The Bedroom*, 1888. Oil on canvas, 72.4 × 91.3 cm. Van Gogh Museum, Amsterdam (Vincent van Gogh Foundation)

p. 34 Mary Beale, *Sketch of the Artist's Son, Bartholomew Beale, Facing Left*, c. 1660. Oil paint on paper, 32.5 × 24.5 cm. Tate, London. Purchased 2010. Photo Tate

p. 38 Claude Lorrain, *Landscape with David at the Cave of Adullam*, 1658. Oil on canvas, 112 × 185 cm. National Gallery, London/Diomedia

p. 41 Claude Lorrain, *Landscape with David at the Cave of Adullam* (detail), 1658. Oil on canvas, 112 × 185 cm. National Gallery, London/Diomedia

p. 42 Jean-François Millet, *The Wood Sawyers*, 1850–1852. Oil on canvas, 57 × 81 cm. Victoria and Albert Museum, London. Photo The Stapleton Collection/ Bridgeman Images

p. 49 John Singer Sargent, *The Birthday Party*, 1887. Oil on canvas, 61 × 73.7 cm. Minneapolis Institute of Arts, Minneapolis

p. 51 Jean-Baptiste Regnault, *The Origin of Painting: Dibutades Tracing the Portrait of a Shepherd*, 1785. Oil on canvas, 120 × 140 cm. Chateaux de Versailles et de Trianon, Versailles. Photo Gérard Blot/RMN-Grand Palais/Dist. Photo SCALA, Florence

p. 52 Thomas Gainsborough, *The Painter's Daughters chasing a Butterfly*, c. 1756. Oil on canvas, 113.5 × 105 cm. National Gallery, London

p. 55 Hasegawa Tōhaku, *Pine Trees / left hand screen*, 16th century. Pair of six-folded screens, ink on paper, 156.8 × 356 cm. Tokyo National Museum, Tokyo

p. 56 Caspar David Friedrich, *The Grosse Gehege near Dresden*, c. 1832. Oil on canvas, 73.5 × 103 cm. Galerie Neue Meister, Dresden

p. 57 Hilaire-Germain-Edgar Degas, *Beach Scene*, c. 1869–1870. Oil on paper mounted on canvas, 47.5 × 82.9 cm. National Gallery, London

p. 59 Cy Twombly, *Untitled*, 2001. Acrylic, paint, pencil on handmade paper unbound in linen slip, 57 × 76 cm. © Cy Twombly Foundation

p. 63 French School (15th century), *Dame Fortune and victims falling from her wheel*, from Boccaccio's *The Fall of Princes*, 1467. Vellum manuscript. Courtesy University of Glasgow Archives & Special Collections, Hunterian collection, MS Hunter 371 (V.1.8)

p. 64 Berthe Morisot, *In a Park*, c. 1874. Pastel on paper, 91.8 × 72.5 cm. Musée des Beaux-Arts de la Ville de Paris, Petit Palais, Paris. Photo Roger-Viollet/TopFoto

p. 70 Albrecht Dürer, *Great Piece of Turf*, 1503. Watercolour, 40.8 × 31.5 cm. The Albertina Museum, Vienna. Image The Albertina Museum, Vienna

p. 71 Pablo Picasso, *Tête de taureau (Bull's Head)*, 1942. Bicycle seat and handlebars (leather and metal), 33.5 × 43.5 × 19 cm. Musée National d'Art Moderne - Centre Pompidou, Paris. Photo Mathieu Rabeau/RMN-Grand Palais/Dist. Photo SCALA, Florence. © 2026 Succession Picasso/DACS, London

p. 73 A tree in the Karwendel area of the Austrian alps. Photo Wolfgang Lutz Unsplash

p. 76 John Ruskin, *Study of Spray of Dead Oak Leaves*, 1879. Watercolour, bodycolor and ink on paper, 14 × 18 cm. Collection of the Guild of St George/Museums Sheffield

p. 79 Gerhard Altzenbach, *The Eleven Ages of Man*, 1609–1672. Engraving, 33 × 43 cm. Metropolitan Museum of Art, New York; The Elisha Whittelsey Collection, The Elisha Whittelsey fund, 1963 (63.601.21)

p. 80 (left) Rembrandt, *Self-Portrait*, c. 1629. Oil on oak panel, 44.4 × 34.2 cm. The Clowes Collection, 2023.4. Courtesy of the Indianapolis Museum of Art at Newfields

p. 80 (right) Rembrandt, *Self-Portrait in a Flat Cap*, 1642. Oil on panel, 70.4 × 58.8 cm. Royal Collection, London

p. 81 (left) Rembrandt, *Self-Portrait*, 1652. Oil on canvas, 112 × 81.5 cm. Kunsthistorisches Museum, Vienna

p. 81 (right) Rembrandt, *Self-Portrait with Two Circles*, c. 1665–1669. Oil on panel, 114.3 × 94 cm. Kenwood House, London

p. 83 James Abbott McNeill Whistler, *Arrangement in grey and black No. 1*, 1871. Oil on canvas, 144.3 × 163 cm. Musée d'Orsay, Paris

p. 84 Ludolf Bakhuysen, *Warships in a Heavy Storm*, c. 1695. Oil on canvas, 150 × 227 cm. Rijksmuseum, Amsterdam

p. 87 Angelica Kauffmann, *Artist in the Character of Design, Listening to the Inspiration of Poetry*, 1782. Oil on canvas, 61 x 61 cm. Kenwood House, London

p. 90 Jacob van Ruisdael, *The Windmill at Wijk bij Duurstede*, c. 1668–1670. Oil on canvas, 83 × 101 cm. Rijksmuseum, Amsterdam

p. 95 Franz Ludwig Catel, *Schinkel in Naples*, 1824. Oil on canvas, 62 × 49 cm. Nationalgalerie, Berlin, Staatliche Museen zu Berlin

p. 98 Paolo Uccello, *The Battle of San Romano*, c. 1435–1440. Tempera on panel, 180 × 316 cm. Louvre Museum, Paris

p. 99 Painter of central Italy (formerly attributed to Luciano Laurana, c. 1420–1479), *View of an Ideal City*, or *The City of God* (detail), c. 1470. Tempera on panel, 67.7 × 239.4 cm. Galleria Nazionale delle Marche, Urbino

p. 100 Carl Schweninger the Younger, *Gossip in the Salon*, c. 1903. Oil on panel, 47 × 60 cm

p. 101 Georg Friedrich Kersting, *Embroiderer* (detail), 1817. Oil on panel, 47.5 × 36.6 cm. National Museum in Warsaw (MNW), Warsaw

p. 102 Pierre-Auguste Renoir, *Luncheon of the Boating Party*, 1880–1881. Oil on canvas, 13 × 17.5 cm. The Phillips Collection, Washington, D.C.

p. 104 Barbara Hepworth, *Pelagos*, 1946. Part painted elm and strings on an oak base, 43 × 46 × 38.5 cm. Tate, London, Presented by the artist 1964. Photo © Tate. Barbara Hepworth © Bowness

p. 106 Vincent van Gogh, *Roses*, 1890. Oil on canvas, 71 × 90 cm. National Gallery of Art, Washington, D.C.

p. 109 Vincent van Gogh, *Self-Portrait with Bandaged Ear*, 1889. Oil on canvas, 60.5 × 50 cm. The Courtauld Gallery, London

p. 114 Nicolas Poussin, *Self-Portrait*, c. 1630. Red chalk on paper, 25.6 × 19.7 cm. British Museum, London. Photo Impaint/Alamy

p. 115 Nicolas Poussin, *Winter or The Flood*, c. 1660–1664. Oil on canvas, 118 × 160 cm. Louvre Museum, Paris. Photo Album/Alamy

p. 117 Boris Kustodiev, *Boy with Teddy Bear*, 1907. Oil on canvas, 69.2 × 69 cm. State Tretyakov Gallery, Moscow

p. 119 Caspar David Friedrich, *The Sea of Ice*, 1823–1824. Oil on canvas, 96.7 × 126.9 cm. Hamburger Kunsthalle, Hamburg

p. 121 Richard Serra, *Fernando Pessoa*, 2007–2008. Weatherproof steel, 300 × 900 × 20.3 cm. Photo Joshua M. White. Courtesy Gagosian. © 2026 Estate of Richard Serra /DACS

p. 124 Workshop of Andrea del Verrocchio, *Tobias and the Angel*, 1470–1475. Tempera on wood, 83.6 × 66 cm. National Gallery, London

p. 129 Helen Allingham, *Old Cottages at Pinner*, 1885–1895. Watercolour on paper, 34.5 x 43 cm. Photo Birmingham Museums Trust, licensed under CC0

p. 133 Raffaello Sanzio, *The School of Athens* (detail), 1509–1511. Charcoal and white lead, 285 × 804 cm. Pinacoteca Ambrosiana, Milan.

p. 135 Giorgio Morandi, *Still Life, Natura Morta*, 1953. Oil on canvas, 30 × 40 cm. Photo Christie's Images/ Bridgeman Images. © 2026 DACS

p. 136 Fantasy image of a Mars Base. Photo Corepics Vof/ Dreamstime.com

p. 137 Pieter Bruegel the Elder, *The Tower of Babel*, 1563. Oil on panel, 114.4 × 155.5 cm. Kunsthistorisches Museum, Vienna

p. 138 Caspar David Friedrich, *The Wanderer Above the Sea of Fog*, c. 1817–1818. Oil on canvas, 98 × 74 cm. Hamburger Kunsthalle, Hamburg

p. 139 Cristiano Ronaldo in action at the Spanish Cup match between FC Barcelona and Real Madrid, Barcelona, January 25, 2012. Photo Natursports/Dreamstime.com

p. 140 Jacques-Louis David, *Napoleon Crossing the Alps or Bonaparte at the St Bernard Pass*, c. 1800–1801. Oil on canvas, 259 × 221 cm. Château de Malmaison, Rueil-Malmaison

p. 141 A Jaguar car. Photo Mateusz Delegacz/Unsplash

p. 142 Unknown sculptor, *Winged Victory* or *Nike of Samothrace*, c. 200–190 BCE. Parian marble, height: 244 cm. Louvre Museum, Paris

p. 147 Pieter de Hooch, *The Courtyard of a House in Delft*, 1658. Oil on canvas, 73 × 60 cm. National Gallery, London

p. 149 Francisco de Zurbarán, *Still Life with Lemons, Oranges and a Rose*, 1633. Oil on canvas, 60 cm × 107 cm. Norton Simon Museum, Pasadena. Photo GL Archive/Alamy

p. 151 Christen Købke, *View of Østerbro from Dosseringen*, 1838. Oil on canvas, 39.5 × 50.5 cm. Kunst Museum Winterthur, Stiftung Oskar Reinhart. Photo © SIK-ISEA, Zürich (Philipp Hitz)

p. 153 Gustave Caillebotte, *Young Man at His Window*, 1875. Oil on canvas, 117 × 82 cm. The J. Paul Getty Museum, Los Angeles, 2021.67. Digital image courtesy of Getty's Open Content Program

p. 155 Agnes Martin, *Wheat*, 1964. Pen and black ink and white gouache, 30 × 30 cm. National Gallery of Art, Washington D.C. © 2026 Agnes Martin Foundation, New York/DACS

p. 156 Buddhist statue of Guanyin, Shanxi province, China, Jin dynasty, 1115–1234. Wood and pigments, 110.7 × 77.6 × 57.4 cm. National Gallery of Victoria, Melbourne, Felton Bequest, 1939. Image courtesy NGV, Melbourne. Photo Christian Markel/NGV

p. 159 Caspar Netscher, *The Lace Maker*, 1662. Oil on canvas, 33 × 27 cm. Photo © Wallace Collection, London /Bridgeman Images

p. 160 Jacques-Louis David, *Belisarius Begging for Alms*, 1781. Oil on canvas, 312 × 288 cm. Palais des Beaux-Arts, Lille

p. 167 Jean Auguste Dominique Ingres, *Henry IV Receiving the Spanish Ambassador*, 1817. Oil on canvas, 39.5 x 50 cm. Petit Palais, Paris

p. 168 Jacques Boulbene, *Henry IV, King of France and Navarre*, c. 1600. Oil on canvas. Musée des Augustins, Toulouse

p. 172 Duncan Grant, a painted pottery dish, c. 1930. Private Collection. Photo David Herbert. © 2026 Estate of Duncan Grant. All rights reserved, DACS

p. 173 The Bloomsbury Set at Charleston farmhouse, in Sussex, England, 1928. Tate, London. Part of the Vanessa Bell Collection, Tate Archive. Presented by Angelica Garnett 1981 and 1988-92. Photo Tate © Tate

p. 176 Antique Windsor Chair. Photo Maryann Preisinger/Dreamstime.com

p. 176 Louis XV Winged Fireside Bergere. Photo Anna Sowa/Alamy

p. 177 Black Leather Armchair. Photo Vadym Andrushchenko/Alamy

p. 177 A simple fork. Photo Andrey Elkin/Alamy Stock Photo

p. 178 (top) An elaborate fork. Photo Igor Kovalchuk /Alamy Stock Photo

p. 178 (bottom) A decorative fork. Photo tarzhanova/123RF.com

ALSO AVAILABLE FOR CHILDREN FROM THE SCHOOL OF LIFE

Big Ideas for Curious Minds

An introduction to philosophy

Children are, in many ways, born philosophers. Without prompting, they ask some of the largest questions: about time, mortality, happiness and the meaning of it all. Yet sadly, too often, this inborn curiosity is not developed and, with age, the questions fall away.

Big Ideas for Curious Minds is designed to harness children's spontaneous philosophical instinct and to develop it through introductions to some of the most vibrant and essential philosophical ideas of history. The book takes us to meet leading figures of philosophy from around the world and from all eras – and shows us how their ideas continue to matter.

ISBN: 978-1-9997471-4-5

ALSO AVAILABLE FOR CHILDREN FROM THE SCHOOL OF LIFE

Big Ideas from History

A history of the world for you

The present can loom very large in a child's mind: all the challenges of the modern world can feel overwhelming and, at times, dispiriting. *Big Ideas from History* is an immense story of what has happened through time, from the beginnings of the universe to now, that speaks personally and constructively to a growing mind.

The book encourages children to think about how and why they experience the world as they do and offers a helpful perspective by placing their thoughts and feelings in the context of our history. What might the dinosaurs or the ancient Egyptians, the Aztec warriors or the Enlightenment thinkers of the 18th century, tell us that could be interesting and useful to hear now? The book also looks to the future and asks the reader to imagine a world they would like to live in. It is a thoughtful and inspiring introduction to the world around us, which encourages the child to engage with themselves and others through history.

ISBN: 978-1-912891-80-1

ALSO AVAILABLE FOR CHILDREN FROM THE SCHOOL OF LIFE

Big Ideas from Science

How scientific discoveries shape our lives

Science is all around us, helping to explain the ideas that matter in our life. By asking questions about how things work, we can gain a deeper understanding of the world and our place in it.

Big Ideas from Science introduces children to some of the most influential scientists throughout history, and the amazing scientific breakthroughs that have changed the way we live – from the discovery of bronze to the invention of the microscope. With engaging facts and playful illustrations, children are encouraged to follow their innate curiosity, to look at the world in different ways and to try and make sense of it.

The book shows us how science not only helps us invent incredible new technology, understand the structure of atoms or reach the moon, but how it can also help us with some of the most important questions in our lives: how can I become a wiser person, a better friend and a kinder, more compassionate human?

ISBN: 978-1-9167531-2-9

ALSO AVAILABLE FOR CHILDREN FROM THE SCHOOL OF LIFE

Big Ideas from Literature

How books can change your world

From an early age, we tend to be told that books matter, but very rarely are we properly allowed to examine why – and therefore we can miss out on a genuine engagement with books. *Big Ideas from Literature* dares to ask the obvious but crucial questions about the whole business of reading: what is reading really for? What are stories trying to do for us? Why should we care?

In a tone that's engaging and playful, we're shown how books help us to grow, why we cry about the fate of certain characters, and how to read for genuine pleasure rather than to please a teacher or parent. Along the way, we learn about the history of literature and about some of the many fascinating books from around the world we might enjoy.

Always, the underlying concern is to foster a love of reading, while appreciating that this might require us to first bluntly question why we should even bother. *Big Ideas from Literature* helps us with the greatest challenge we can ever have around books: how to make them into our true friends.

ISBN: 978-1-915087-48-5

THE SCHOOL OF LIFE

The School of Life is a global organisation helping people lead more fulfilled lives. It is a resource for helping us understand ourselves, for improving our relationships, our careers and our social lives – as well as for helping us find calm and get more out of our leisure hours.

We do this through films, workshops, books and gifts – and provide a warm and supportive community. You can find us online, in stores and in welcoming spaces around the globe.

ANDY WARHOL